SELL YOUR HOME WITH CONFIDENCE

SELL YOUR HOME WITH CONFIDENCE: REDUCE YOUR LIABILITY WHEN SELLING

Copyright © 2018 by Saman Saba

This book or any portion thereof may not be reproduced or used in any manner whatsoever, without the express written permission of the author, except for the use of brief quotations in a review.

DISCLAIMER: The information contained within this book should not be considered legal advice and is for informational purposes only. Additionally, no client-attorney relationship has been established.

For more information, write to: support@samansaba.com

Paperback ISBN: 978-1-7322710-0-5
Kindle ISBN: 978-1-7322710-1-2

SELL YOUR HOME WITH CONFIDENCE

Reduce Your Liability When Selling

SAMAN SABA

FREE
MASTERCLASS

The #1 Legal Document Every Real Estate Seller & Buyer
Needs To Draft As Soon As They Make The Decision To
Sell Or Buy

DEDICATION

———— ❖ ————

To my parents.

Without your unconditional love, selflessness, and support, this book would not be possible.

You mean everything to me.

TABLE OF CONTENTS

❖

PREFACE

❖

WHY I WROTE THIS BOOK

❝ *The real estate industry is incredibly transparent, ethical, and litigious-free."*

Said no one.

Ever.

Before we begin, we should be very clear about reality. For too long, consumers have been left in the dark in regards to what they *can* and *should* expect during the sale of their home. As a result, homeowners have been left expecting the bare minimum while having their guards up, ready for something, *anything*, to go wrong at a moment's notice. But there is a simpler alternative, and it all begins with you and this book.

This book is a culmination of my first-hand experience, while practicing as both a real estate attorney and real estate agent, which has positioned me to make several key observations about the industry. During this time, it has become evident that there is a need for sellers to be armed with proper information that can help reduce their liabilities - because without trying to sound too cliché, sellers simply don't know what they don't know. However, this is through no fault of their own. In fact, after poring over the available books, I found that while the topic has certainly been addressed, there isn't nearly enough cohesive and comprehensive information that clearly delineates how sellers can minimize their exposure to litigation.

This is why I wrote this book - I believe that in order for you to avoid disappointment during (and after) the selling process, it is critical to educate yourself as much as possible. This is why in my real estate practice, my number one priority is to educate my clients. In doing so, I take the approach of asking myself, *"What if everyone knew what I know about real estate?"* With this question in mind, I believe I have developed a finely tuned approach that has potentially saved my clients

1

thousands of dollars by avoiding litigation. Now, I want to share that approach with you in this book. In fact, when I often speak to home sellers and share with them the things I will share with you in this book, they are shocked to learn that no one had ever bothered to share it with them before. However, this really should not be too much of a surprise. After all, there are real estate agents out there right now who are fighting to protect their old-fashioned business models, which run parallel to keeping certain information under lock and key and I will be discussing these agents and their unscrupulous practices in Part Two of this book.

With this book, I hope to push back the curtain and reveal what is happening behind-the-scenes in the real estate industry so that consumers can make more knowledgeable and profitable decisions regarding the sale of their home. The truth between these pages will bring us all one step closer to challenging the status quo and empowering individual homeowners and sellers. You see, when we are armed with the profound clarity of what is expected of our chosen real estate professionals, only then can we begin to hold the entire industry to a higher standard. And hopefully, in turn and in due time, we can slowly but surely begin to build a relationship with our chosen professional that is rooted in trust rather than suspicion.

In fact, I firmly believe that the insight provided to you in this book will lead to a smoother transaction between you and your buyer. Specifically, when you take into account all the ways that the sale of your home can expose you to litigation, you inherently do the right thing as you are now empowered by your newly acquired insight. But also, the information in this book will lead to a more trusting relationship between you and your real estate professional. This is because when the real estate professional knows that the homeowner is aware of what is expected of them, the professional will also choose to do the right thing, which inherently and clearly leads the homeowner to trust their professional.

And make no mistake about it, trust is an incredible thing. Extraordinary things happen when we can all trust one another, and the same especially applies when we are able to trust the people who help us sell our home. Simon Sinek, a renowned motivational speaker and author recently addressed the topic of trust in a TED Talk. He began by saying how thousands of years ago, the world was full of varying forces that were out to kill us, and as a result, humans became social animals. We worked together to look after one another and trusted one another as the bedrock of our personal survival. We entrusted our community with our children as we left to hunt or explore, knowing that the community would protect our family upon our return. Therefore, trust was an incredibly important factor in the advancement of our entire species. Similarly, trust can be an important factor in changing the course of the real estate industry - to push it forward. When we add trust to the equation, we remove unnecessary stress and headache, which only leads us towards smoother transactions.

Speaking of trust, I recognize that you have put your trust in me by purchasing this book, and I consider it a privilege that you have decided to spend your time reading it. As such, it is my full intention to not waste your time, but rather, equip you with just the right amount of information to help empower your decisions regarding the sale of your property. I know that you are busy and that you may not share my passion of real estate, but perhaps, like myself, you are viscerally drawn to seeking out the truth. That's a world I naturally live in, and the reason I decided to attend law school. Because I believe that the truth will always be revealed. Or, like my mother who always reminded me as a child with the Persian proverb, "The moon never stays behind the cloud." In other words, sooner or later, the truth comes out, just like the moon.

Further, I believe that regardless of what industry you operate in, if there are inherent flaws within it, it is your duty and responsibility to expose them. As Edmund Burke so eloquently once said:

"All that is necessary for the triumph of evil is that good men do nothing."

There comes a time that if you don't speak out about a problem, then you become part of that problem. This book is my way of speaking out. As you will see in Part Two of this book, I will be exposing hidden truths and behaviors that I view as unethical so that you can be vigilant about hiring an ethical professional.

I believe this is important information for you to know because when we are talking about the single largest investment of your life, ignorance is not bliss. And for this simple reason alone, I know I will face some criticism for writing this book - because I am exposing the "secrets of real estate practitioners."

> **It is easy to see why some real estate agents don't want their clients privy to certain pieces of information - let's face it, it is in the best interests of some agents for you to not be aware of all the ways that they can take advantage of you.**

Now, to clarify, what I will be sharing with you may not be actual "secrets," per se, but they are tidbits of information that are definitely unbeknownst or unclear to many sellers. And as a result of not being privy to or fully understanding this information, many unethical real estate professionals have been able to take advantage of sellers and line their own pocketbooks by making a quick sale. Therefore, the goal of this book is to demystify the real estate industry for the seller.

Now, don't get me wrong, this book is not an attack on the real estate industry or real estate agents. By sharing these "secrets" with you, my goal is not to make a sweeping generalization that all real estate agents behave in unethical and dishonest manners. In fact, I've had the pleasure of working with many agents who've had to make hard choices, but have chosen to do right by their clients. And of course, without a doubt, these agents were also able to guide sellers through the process with more ease than if a seller were to go through the home selling process alone.

But like almost every single industry, real estate also has their fair share of shady practitioners. These agents are prepared to twist the rules to their own advantage. These agents have a painfully discernible pattern behind everything they say and do. These agents leave innocent home sellers questioning whether they hired the right agent, one with their best interests in mind. These agents often make decisions that benefit their bottom line, at the cost of yours.

But a lack of ethics and wondering whether money is being left on the table are just symptoms of a much greater problem - many home sellers are failing to properly educate themselves despite the fact that we are in the midst of living in a more transparent world every day. With the advent of information technology, more and more information becomes readily available, which has led many home sellers to be faced with information overload.

Collins Dictionary defines informational overload as, "the situation when someone has so much information that they are unable to deal with it." Further, David Lewis, a psychologist once said:

"Having too much information can be as dangerous as having too little. Among other problems, information overload can lead to a paralysis of analysis, making it far harder to find the right solutions."

Clearly, due to the tremendous amount of information available to sellers, it can be difficult to sift through all the data and pick up only the pertinent pieces. That is why I wrote this book; I have done all the heavy lifting for you, and I have included all the pertinent information a home seller would generally need to greatly reduce their chances of facing litigation after their property has been sold.

If you are thinking about selling your home, this book will help you save time and energy by avoiding legal headaches. Furthermore, it will help keep more money in your pocket now AND after you have sold your home, as you can rest assured that you have taken the right steps in avoiding the costs associated with litigation. I have done my best to keep this book as short as possible, while still conveying a full and detailed breadth of knowledge. Therefore, this book is broken down into just two major parts.

1. In Part One we will take a deep look at the top ways home sellers expose themselves to litigation and what you can do to reduce your exposure.
2. In Part Two, we will discuss what you can expect from a real

estate professional, the benefits of working with one, and the differences between hiring an agent versus a real estate attorney.

It is therefore my hope that each and every one of you will share this book with your own circle of loved ones, so that all homeowners can see the truth for themselves, which I believe will finally close the chapter on many unethical practices. It is my sincerest hope that you will find the information within these pages insightful and illuminating, as you prepare to sell your home. More importantly, it is my hope that you understand the power in knowledge, because the sale of your home is a journey, and as such, I hope you use this book as a reliable GPS that will help you reach your desired destination safely and lawsuit free!

To your success!
Saman Saba, Esq.

INTRODUCTION

❖

It goes without saying that the first step in the home selling process is making the decision to sell. What I have found in my practice, however, is that there are a plethora of reasons that spark the idea of selling in a homeowner's mind. For some, this decision will be difficult and emotional. For others, the decision will come quite readily.

Sometimes, when a homeowner receives a job transfer, gets a new job or simply finds the daily commute unbearable, he or she will often make the decision to sell and purchase a property closer to his or her workplace. Other reasons for relocating include being closer to friends or family, the desire to live in a different city or a better part of town, or simply wanting better amenities. Other reasons include having a growing (or shrinking) family, facing personal hardships such as divorce, death, or health related issues, or wanting your children to be enrolled in a better school system.

Regardless of your reason to sell, one thing is absolutely certain: if you are considering moving, you are not alone. According to the U.S. Census Bureau, more than 40 million Americans decide to move each year. However, knowing you are not alone does not mitigate the fact that, compared to buying a home, selling a home is a downright emotionally draining process. For those selling out of necessity or hardship, the emotional toll can be even greater.

I have observed that many homeowners greatly underestimate the challenges involved in the selling process. First, you have to get your home ready to sell by completing minor repairs. This means you will be spending money on a home you will no longer own, which can be a bit frustrating. Then, you have to deal with the whole selling process - setting the price, having your home 'show-ready' at all times, negotiating the sale, and so much more. And to top it all off, you still have to pack up your entire house and relocate.

While the to-do list seems never ending to a prospective seller, it is unfortunate that more home sellers do not begin with the most paramount task of all: educating themselves in ways to avoid litigation. Home sellers often gloss over their exposure to risk, because they believe that by virtue of hiring a real estate advisor, their risk somehow evaporates. However, as you will come to see, while a trusted advisor can be worth their weight in gold, some advisors can cause more harm than good — which is why it is imperative to know how to hire a *true* professional among a sea of rookies.

As you go through this book, you will see that selling a home is not as simple as putting it on the market, getting an offer, and moving out. There are so many more decisions that will need to be made for a successful sale. I have provided you with a guideline of steps to take, and some problems that you may experience. With that being said, I have included some information that is applicable to the state of Maryland. However, it is important to note that each state has its own set of rules and you should always consult with an attorney, and that none of the information contained in this book should be construed as legal advice.

PART ONE:

TOP SELLER NIGHTMARES

CHAPTER ONE

❖

SELLER NIGHTMARE #1: FAILURE TO DISCLOSE

You have decided to sell.

Now what?

Now is about the time when reality begins to set in. You realize that the process of selling your home begins with major decisions that can legally impact you in major ways, *for yeeeeeeeeeeeeears* to come. But don't worry; I've got you covered! By reading this book, you will be armed with the information and tools necessary to avoid unnecessary expenses, stress, and potential lawsuits.

Full and proper disclosure by a seller is a critical aspect of every home sale. Think of it like this: a doctor walks into the examination room and provides a patient with a diagnosis of the patient's health. The doctor is in a position of authority, because he or she has spent years studying medicine and the human anatomy. This encourages the patient to defer to the doctor's knowledge and perhaps rely on the advice of the doctor.

In turn, when a seller discloses problems about specific aspects of the property, the seller is providing a diagnosis regarding the health of their property. Consequently, buyers will defer to the seller's knowledge of the property, since they will view the seller as a person with the authority to speak on these issues. As such, a buyer will be relying on the seller's disclosures when the buyer decides to purchase the home. If a seller fails to properly disclose, I can attest to the fact that the likely prognosis will be litigation.

The number one reason sellers find themselves in a legal nightmare is because they fail to reveal material facts about the home that impact the value or desirability. However, this issue can be easily resolved if sellers simply changed their perspective on disclosures.

Unfortunately, many home sellers believe that disclosures burden them, while solely protecting the buyer. The truth is, disclosures serve to protect both sides of the transaction. While disclosures certainly protect the buyer from purchasing a lemon, it also protects you from a potential lawsuit. When you properly disclose, the prospective buyer is placed on notice about an issue and if they decide to move forward with the purchase, then you will not be liable for future problems since you gave them an opportunity to investigate. Sadly, many home sellers fail to see it this way.

Many homeowners decide to withhold information due to the belief that prospective buyers will lose interest in the home or will ask for a significant price reduction if they know about every defect.

> **But a better way to think about disclosures is that it is better to lose a potential buyer by being upfront and disclosing all known issues than it is to spend a few years' worth of energy and tens of thousands of dollars in litigation.**

Before we dive into the different types of defects that must be disclosed, as well as possible solutions to protecting yourself from a costly suit, let's briefly examine how state laws treat disclosures.

CHAPTER TWO

❖

STANDARD OF LAW: DUTY TO DISCLOSE OR DISCLAIM

In each state, residential real estate sellers must complete a form in which they can disclaim or disclose (or both!) any known defects with the property to all prospective buyers. In Maryland, according to the Annotated Code of Maryland, Real Property Article, Section 10-702[1], all home sellers must complete a form known as the Residential Property Disclosure and Disclaimer Statement. Since this document must be presented to all buyers before they submit an offer, I have attached the form here for your convenience. https://www.dllr.state. md.us/forms/danddform.doc

As you can see, the Residential Property Disclosure and Disclaimer Statement is in fact two forms: one form allows you to disclose any known defects, and the other allows you to disclaim any knowledge of latent defects. These forms are state-specific, but they are likely very similar to the one attached. Before you decide which form to complete, it may be wise to have your agent or real estate attorney determine which one is more prevalent within your neighborhood. This is important, because a prospective buyer may find it suspicious to purchase a property where that seller is the only one to disclaim, while everyone else has chosen to disclose.

I will discuss how to properly fill out both forms, but regardless of how the form is filled out, the seller should always make disclosures or disclaimers to the buyer in writing.

Additionally, both the buyer and seller

---

[1] Most of the sources in the book will correlate with Maryland law. It is advisable to hire an attorney who is knowledgeable with the state laws applicable within the state your property is located in.

should sign and date the document to confirm acknowledgment of receipt. These two steps are very important since according to the Annotated Code of Maryland, Real Property Article, Section 10-702(h), a buyer who does not acknowledge having received the "disclosure or disclaimer statement on or before entering into the contract of sale has the unconditional right, upon written notice to the vendor or vendor's agent to rescind the contract of sale at any time before the receipt of the disclosure or disclaimer statement or within 5 days following receipt of the disclosure or disclaimer statement and to the immediate return of any deposits made on account of the contract." Thus, in order to mitigate the chances of a buyer rescinding their offer, it is important to give the buyers an opportunity to review the disclosures or disclaimers **before** they submit their offer. By doing so, the disclaimer or disclosure forms are then fully incorporated within the Purchase Agreement from the onset, as they will be submitted as part of the offer with the purchaser signing the bottom of the form.

Moreover, it is a smart move to be familiarized with the Annotated Code of Maryland, Real Property Article, Section 10-702(b), (or your state's equivalent statute) as it expressly and clearly states the different circumstances in which a seller may be eligible to waive disclosure or disclaimer requirements. For example, in a sale of unimproved real property (raw land), and a sale in the course of an administration of a decedent's estate or trust, sellers are not legally obligated to disclose or disclaim. It should also be noted that beyond the very narrow exceptions listed in the law, the buyer and seller may not simply agree that the property is sold is "as-is" with the intention of waiving the need to disclose. In fact, any attempted waiver of disclosing or disclaiming between the parties is deemed void in the eyes of the courts. To be certain that your unique circumstance allows you waive disclaimer or disclosure requirements, it is always advisable to consult with an attorney in your state.

DISCLOSING

If you choose to disclose, you will need to answer either "yes," "no," or "unknown" to a set of questions pertaining to the condition of the property - including everything from the roof down to the basement, and everything in between. Additionally, as you can see, the questions also address some potential issues that cannot be found with the naked eye. These issues include zoning matters, HOA restrictions, recorded/ unrecorded easements, as well as several others.

To be clear, it is perfectly acceptable for the seller of a home to answer a question as "unknown." The purpose of the disclosure is to inform the buyer what is known about the property, not to initiate a full-blown investigation. There is also a space provided below each question allowing a seller the opportunity to give details on defects or other issues. If there is not enough space provided on the form, the seller may supplement it with a list of additional information. While completing this form, it can be helpful for sellers to utilize the comments area below each question to further explain a situation. For example, one question asks whether the property is located on a flood zone. If the seller answers "yes," this can compel the buyer to not place an offer. However, perhaps the seller recently submitted an appeal and has received a notice stating the flood zone was amended, and as such, the property will no longer be deemed to be in a flood zone in the upcoming year. In light of this information, a potential buyer may now have the information they needed to move forward with an offer.

Also, when answering the forms, note that *a half-truth is a full lie.* In other words, if a seller makes a representation that is only half true, and the seller knows that the information provided will be misleading absent full disclosure of additional facts, the seller can be found liable. For example, some sellers may intentionally be vague in their answers by stating, "we have done no work that requires permits since owning the property" when the seller is fully aware that the previous owner had completed work, yet failed to obtain the proper permits. Moreover, if the work was disclosed to a seller when he or she purchased the property, then the seller should bear in mind that there is probably a paper trail that can prove that the information is inaccurate, which can come back to haunt the seller, especially in our increasingly technologically advanced world. Additionally, the buyers could cross check disclosures with the city building permit and zoning reports. Therefore, sellers should always make disclosures in good faith while being fully honest and unambiguous.

DISCLAIMING

Alternatively, if a seller decides to disclaim, he or she does not have to use the checklist form in detail. Rather, a seller may simply state that he or she does not have knowledge of any material latent defects, if this is a true and accurate statement. According to the Annotated Code of Maryland, Real Property Article, Section 10-702, a seller must "disclose any latent defects of which the [seller] has *actual knowledge* that a purchaser would not reasonably be expected to ascertain by a careful visual inspection and that would pose a direct threat to the health or safety of the purchaser or an occupant." Therefore, if a seller has knowledge about something that the buyer cannot discover by a reasonable examination of the property, then the seller must disclose that information.

So now, you may be wondering, what is defined as *actual* knowledge of a defect in the eyes of the courts?

In a situation where the seller did not know that there was a defect since he or she did not live in the house for long, or if he or she was simply unobservant, then there may be no fraud or misrepresentation and thus, no liability. The difficulty for buyers in proving such an action lies in the determination of whether the seller was aware of the defect. For example, if a defect was hidden behind the walls or beneath the floors, and only came to light when the walls and flooring were removed for renovations, then it is reasonable to believe that the sellers were not aware and thus, would not be liable for nondisclosure. In Maryland, a seller is only responsible for disclosing those defects of which he or she is aware. Thus, by choosing to complete the disclaimer form, it does not alleviate you from your duty of disclosing *latent* defects.

So now, what's defined as a *latent* defect?

We will discuss the different types of defects in more detail in the upcoming chapter. But before we move on, there is one critical point that must be addressed and fully understood by all sellers.

> **In fact, if there is just ONE thing that you take away from this chapter, it is this: if you decide to work with an agent, he or she has a profound legal obligation to pass along any pertinent information regarding any defects that you may have shared with them to the buyers and their representatives.**

Failure to do to so may render your agent without a license to practice real estate through disciplinary action that can be brought against them by the buyers.

To illustrate this, imagine you tell your agent that whenever it rains more than 4 inches, water leaks into the basement, but you do not want to disclose this information to prospective buyers. While as the seller, you do not want to share this information with the buyers, Maryland law *requires* real estate licensees, including attorneys, to disclose any material facts that the licensees know or should have known.

Perhaps you are thinking, *but what about the attorney-client confidentiality privilege? Does that not apply?*

According to Black's Law Dictionary, the attorney-client privilege is defined as a "right an individual has for the information he gives his attorney that it be kept confidential." Now, although confidentiality is the bedrock of our legal system, as it encourages clients to communicate fully and frankly with their lawyers, the duty to disclose to prospective buyers outweighs an attorney blindly following orders from their client to remain silent regarding a material defect. A case in point is when a client tell his lawyer that he intends to lie on the witness stand and thereby, the attorney is torn between his duty of confidentiality and his duty of candor towards the tribunal. In deciding how to handle the situation, according to American Bar Association's Center for Professional Responsibility, the Rules of Professional Conduct 1.6 states, "an attorney may reveal information relating to the representation of the client to the extent the lawyer reasonably believes necessary to prevent the client from committing fraud that is reasonably certain to result in substantial injury to the financial interest or property of another and in furtherance of which the client has used or is using the lawyer's services." Therefore, under such circumstances, a lawyer must encourage their client to be truthful and, where appropriate, the attorney may withdraw his or her representation of that client.

However, there is a distinction between disclosure of defects and disclosure of a seller's motivation behind their desire to selling. Your motivations behind the desire to sell your property are always protected, and your attorney or agent should not share this information with prospective buyers, unless you consent to disclosure. For example, if you are getting divorced or having financial trouble and need to sell your home quickly, this fact should always be kept confidential by your representative.

Now, let's examine the different types of defects that must be disclosed.

CHAPTER THREE

❖

THE DIFFERENT TYPES OF DEFECTS

Many homeowners have difficulty deciding which defects should or should not be disclosed. Generally, sellers must disclose any "material" facts about the property, which include any information that could impact the price of the property, or influence a prospective buyer's decision to purchase a home. Clearly, this is a subjective standard, since a fact can be viewed as material by one buyer but not to another.

A good rule of thumb to use when deciding whether certain information should be disclosed or not is this: *if you have to ask whether or not you should disclose it, you should disclose it*. Or put differently, you should follow the old adage of, "treat others the way you would want to be treated." Ask yourself, "*If I was purchasing a home, would I want the sellers to share this information with me?*" Usually, that answer is a resounding, "YES!" Following this rule could save you a lot of trouble down the road.

Under the law, there are two types of defects that you should disclose: patent defects and latent defects. Before we get into these types of defects, I should make it clear that even if something does not fall under the category of a latent or patent defect, the seller may still be found to be on the hook. For example, sellers have a duty to disclose accurate information about a property, including square footage, which can be a tricky element to categorize as either patent or latent. Although most Multiple Listing Services (MLS) use language along the lines of, "information deemed reliable but not guaranteed," if you have reason to know that the square footage is grossly mistaken, you have a duty to disclose this fact.

Now, a patent defect is a defect that is apparent when a buyer walks into a home. For instance, there could be a deteriorating deck, or a broken window, or some other defect that is obvious to any person who is conducting a routine home inspection. Therefore, a patent defect is governed by the legal doctrine of *caveat emptor*, which is Latin for "let the buyer beware." More specifically, this doctrine implicates that the buyer alone is responsible for checking the quality and suitability of goods before a purchase is made, which is done through an inspection.

While it is true that buyers should "beware" when it comes to the purchase of a residential property, this defense does not go very far in the eyes of the courts. By merely allowing the buyer to conduct a home inspection, the seller cannot use the defense of *caveat emptor*, since there are limitations as to what an inspector can uncover during a home inspection, such as latent defects.

Furthermore, the <u>Annotated Code of Maryland, Real Property Article, Section 10-702</u>, defines 'latent defects' to mean "material defects in real property or an improvement ... that: (1) a purchaser would not reasonably be expected to ascertain or observe by a careful visual inspection of the real property; and (2) would pose a direct threat to the health or safety of: (i) the purchaser; or (ii) an occupant of the real property ."

Therefore, a latent defect includes hidden defects that could not have been discovered by a reasonably thorough inspection before the sale, which leaves the buyers having to accept the sellers' word for any potential underlying problems. These are also the types of defects that most home sellers often fail to disclose, which is why the courts have refused to recognize the validity of the *caveat emptor* defense. In cases where the seller knows of any material latent defect that makes the home uninhabitable, unfit, or dangerous, they ***must*** disclose this defect to the buyer.

Obviously, you don't have to disclose every little scratch on the floor or stain on the counter of the home you're selling. But you should disclose other types of defects. To give you a better idea of what you should disclose, here is a list of the different types of defects home sellers often fail to disclose.

- Water leaks of any kind, such as leaks in the basement, roof, or around windows

- Plumbing, drainage, and sewage issues
- Unstable foundation or cracks in the foundation
- Faulty electrical wiring
- Termites or other insect or pest infestation
- Roof defects
- Heating or air conditioning system issues
- Toxic hazards in the house such as mold, lead, mildew, radon, mercury, carbon monoxide, or asbestos
- Environmental hazards, like if the property is located in or around a flood plain, wetland, landfill, underground pit, or other earth-stability defects
- Problems with title, such as unregistered easements and pending litigation
- Neighbor disputes or nuisances such as noise, odor, smoke, and agricultural nuisances
- Boundary issues
- Improperly completed owner repairs, construction defects
- Whether the home is in a special historic district (as it will affect a purchaser's ability to make repairs)
- Whether the home is governed by a homeowner's association (HOA)

It is important to note that, while there is nothing wrong with wanting to make sure your home is show-ready, you cannot intentionally conceal what would otherwise be a patent defect. For example, if you paint over water spots or mold, or patch up signs of structural movement such as cracks to the foundation, you could open yourself up to a lawsuit. When you attempt to deliberately conceal a problem, those problems will likely re-appear at a later time, thus setting the stage for a lawsuit. Even something as simple as trying o cover up worn out hardwood floors with a floor rug is a bad idea.

> Bottom line, buyers do not like surprises, just as much as you don't like lawsuits.

STIGMATIZED PROPERTIES

Now, close your eyes and think back to when you were a kid. Do you remember that one run-down house at the end of the street? The one that was rumored to have been haunted? Well, in addition to having to disclose latent defects, in some states, you may have to also disclose the history regarding a property, especially if the property has become stigmatized because of a rumor, like the house being haunted. Stigmatized properties are those that society has found undesirable, not because of a physical (latent or patent) defect, but because of the sometimes strong psychological reaction it may elicit among buyers, if assuming that they were to know about the defect.

In regards to haunted homes, Maryland does not currently have a pointed decision from the courts expressly declaring the existence of "ghosts" as a material fact that requires disclosure. However, since the courts have generally held that a material fact is anything that *might* impact the prospective buyer's decision to purchase, or their offering price, I would suggest that any knowledge of rumors regarding the property being "haunted" to be disclosed. Of course, someone's opinion that a property is haunted does not necessarily constitute a fact; therefore, before you decide to disclose that the property is haunted, be certain that a fact has indeed been established first. This bring us to our next point, regarding properties in which a death or crime has occurred.

In some states, certain events, including criminal activity, prostitution, homicide/suicide, and illegal drug manufacturing, are required to be disclosed. However, under Maryland law, Annotated Code of Maryland, Real Property Article, Section 2-120, these are explicitly excluded. With this said, bear in mind that if a prospective buyer specifically asks about these issues, and you are aware that they did in fact occur, you cannot lie. On the other hand, a disclosure that a previous owner or occupant had AIDS or was HIV positive is not a material fact or a latent defect relating to property offered for sale or lease. Furthermore, according to health law policy, such information is deemed protected information, which further bolsters why it should not be disclosed.

But even if a particular disclosure is not legally required, if you have a piece of information about a house that a prospective buyer may not like, you should disclose it anyway. This is especially true for patent and latent defects, because buyers can almost always get their neighbors to talk. For example, maybe the neighbor had the same exact problem that was not disclosed, or maybe the neighbor saw plumbing contractors in your driveway several times. Or, maybe, by dumb luck, you had a contractor come look at the problem, and then the buyer contacts the same exact contractor who notifies them that they were at that same property for that same issue just months prior. Whether it is the neighbor or the contractor, these individuals can be considered as first hand witnesses who can testify in a court of law to what they saw.

Either way, when it comes to disclosures, it is always better to be safe than sorry. This is particularly why it is important that your agent or attorney has a strong grasp of the laws relating to what needs to be disclosed. If you sense that your chosen professional does not fully understand or comprehend the laws pertaining to proper disclosure, it may be wise to consider finding another professional so that they don't take a misstep that can then open you up to liability, better known as vicarious liability. Of course, we will dive into vicarious liability later on, but for now it is important for you to take the time to understand the basics of real estate law so that you will know how to answer a question properly and honestly when asked.

CHAPTER FOUR

— ❖ —

SELLING "AS-IS" IS NOT A SOLUTION

M any homeowners have misconceptions regarding selling their property "as-is." As mentioned earlier, the buyer and seller are not legally entitled to agreeing that the property will be sold "as-is" in an attempt to circumspect the seller's duty to disclose or disclaim. Furthermore, mistakenly, homeowners think that deciding to sell "as-is" exonerates them from their duty to disclose known defects not otherwise observable to a buyer. And unfortunately, these sellers are under the false impression that they can unload the property for a lower price while avoiding the need to disclose known issues regarding the home. However, as we will explore now, selling "as-is" does not relieve you from your legal duty to disclose.

More accurately, selling a home in an "as-is" condition simply allows prospective buyers to know that while they are welcome to and have a right to conduct an inspection, the sellers will not be willing to make any repairs to the property. In other words, what you see is what you get.

I usually advise homeowners against advertising that their property is being sold "as-is" from the onset. This is because, when a property is advertised "as-is," a potential buyer, often an uneducated buyer, will automatically construe this to mean that there may indeed be problems with the home. In fact, they may assume that there is something seriously wrong with the property, perhaps too expensive to be fixed or not fixable at all which is why you have decided to sell the home "as-is" in the first place!

Although the buyer may or may not be accurate in their determination, these prospective buyers have now discounted the value of your home and as a result, they will more likely than not be more inclined to submitting a low-ball offer. Additionally, since buyers will assume that there is something wrong with the property, you will attract fewer buyers. These factors, taken together with the fact that many sellers often already list below market value when selling "as-is," will often leave you netting a lot less than if you had not advertised your property "as-is" from the onset.

Further, assuming that you do receive a reasonable offer and you accept it, be prepared that most buyers will still try to re-negotiate the sales price after the inspector's report comes in, especially if the report reveals that there are indeed expensive repairs needed to make the property habitable. As the seller, you are able to then re-establish the fact that the property is sold "as-is", re-negotiate the sales price, or provide a repair escrow. Again, although you may be inclined to advertise your property "as-is" from the start, I think a better tactic would be to hold off until after you have begun negotiations with a prospective buyer. Let me explain.

If you list your home for $500,000 and the buyer negotiates you down to $450,000, you might find yourself feeling that you are giving the buyer an incredible deal on your home and thus, during the final round of negotiations, you may tell the buyer or the buyer's agent that the home is being sold "as-is." Meaning, you would not be willing to provide any further seller concessions in the form of either re-negotiating the price or making any repairs for any defects. Thus, when the negotiation process between a buyer and seller becomes arduous, I suggest keeping the option of selling your property "as-is" as a back pocket negotiation strategy.

On a final note, let's assume that you and the buyer were moving along towards settlement until the inspection report reveals a previously unknown material defect, which causes the buyer to not want to move forward. Under this scenario, the buyer, assuming the contract has a "Sell As-Is Inspection" clause, can then cancel their Purchase Agreement, causing you to have to place the property back on the market. In this case, although you may have not known about the defect when you first placed the property on the market, now that you are aware, you should update the property disclosures to reflect any newfound knowledge of latent defects, or else risk being sued. One way this may occur is that the buyer's agent will see that the property is no longer under contract and may ask (1) if there was an inspection conducted and (2) if that inspection uncovered any major defects. When the buyer's agent asks these questions, you, your agent, and/or your attorney will have a duty to respond truthfully.

Regardless of whether or not you decide to sell "as-is," you are legally required to accurately and completely answer the disclosure forms. If you willfully fail to disclose prior problems, a buyer is entitled to recover actual damages (AKA money). Thus, selling "as-is" is not a way to exonerate you from your duty to disclose. However, a tactic that you can use to mitigate any potential lawsuits would be to arm yourself by conducting an inspection before placing your property on the market. Such an inspection is commonly referred to as a pre-listing home inspection, which is what we will discuss in the upcoming chapter.

CHAPTER FIVE

❖

A POSSIBLE SOLUTION:
PRE-LISTING HOME INSPECTIONS

If you are selling your house, consider a home inspection before the house goes on the market, also known as a pre-listing inspection. On the one hand, you may not want to do a pre-listing inspection, because you will have a duty to now disclose any defects that will be revealed in the report. And obviously, these would have been defects that you would ordinarily not have needed to disclose since you were not aware of them before the pre-listing inspection. However, as you will now see, having the knowledge of potential defects can be incredibly empowering for home sellers.

One major way that the knowledge of defects through a pre-listing inspection can empower you as the seller is by giving you the power to decide on how to best repair the defects, both efficiently and cost-effectively, too! It is always cheaper to fix all those little problems yourself than to allow the buyer to find these little defects and then to request them in their list of requested repairs, commonly known as the "Inspection Notice." This is because most, if not all, standard Inspection Notices will require the repairs to be conducted by a licensed contractor. In fact, in Maryland, most forms expressly state that not only must they be conducted by a licensed contractor but the seller must also provide all invoices to the purchaser before settlement as a means of ensuring that the work was completed by a MHIC licensed professional. As for the cost of hiring a professional, as previously mentioned, it would be beneficial for you to have completed the work yourself or a reliable non-licensed handyman. This is largely due to the fact that you are playing approximately 25% to cover the cost associated to the overhead and profit margins for the contractor.

Additionally, since you now know of the defects up front, this gives you the unique ability to make repairs to any defects that were revealed, which may enable you to increase your listing price. As such, you may be able to not only cover the expenses to fix the repairs, but also, you may be able to net more money from the sale. Thus, having conducted a pre-listing home inspection will place you in a stronger negotiating position.

But also, since you have the opportunity to fix major problems ahead of time, you will be able to drastically mitigate the possibility of a buyer overestimating the severity of a needed repair. In turn, you may have potentially saved yourself from experiencing any unnecessary headaches or stress that can come from a buyer demanding costly repairs, price reductions, or worse, abandonment of the sale entirely. Moreover, a seller can use the inspection report to help them avoid a lawsuit after the sale, too. This is because it can be used as evidence to prove that the seller truly did not know, nor should they have known of a particular defect, if a buyer later finds one that was not shown on the inspection report. Clearly, a pre-listing inspection can help avoid surprises and reduce possible negotiation problems.

Finally, when a pre-listing inspection is conducted and the buyers have received a copy of the report, this will undoubtedly be perceived favorably by prospective buyers. Look at it this way: if a seller handed you a copy of an inspection report, wouldn't you telegraph their proactive approach as an honest attempt on their behalf to deliver a property that is in good condition to you? I know I would! In my point of view, it shows me that there is nothing to hide. But of course, I also abide by the old adage, "trust, but verify." As such, as the buyer, I would still conduct my own home inspection, but at least the sellers have given me a warm and fuzzy feeling, knowing that they want to be up front with me.

HIRING AN INSPECTOR

In regards to hiring a qualified inspector, if you are selling your property and need a pre-listing inspection, it is important for you to speak to several different inspectors. You may ask friends or family members who recently purchased a home who they used as their inspector to find the names of some good inspectors. But either way, be sure to ask several important questions to ensure the inspector is qualified.

Some of these questions include:

- May I see a copy of your inspection agreement?
- Do you provide any refunds if not satisfied with the level of inspection?
- Do you offer any warranties?
- May I see a copy of a sample report?
- What exactly will be inspected?
- How much will the service cost?
- Do you offer other services in addition to an inspection?
- Will you be able to perform the repairs?
- What types of inspections do you conduct?
- How long will the inspection take?
- How long until the inspection report is available?
- Do you carry an error and omissions and general liability insurance?
- What happens if you missed an important defect?

Finally, while we are on the topic of inspectors, it is important to note their role in a potential lawsuit. Inspectors are often included as a co-defendant, if a buyer initiates a

> **Also, here is a little tip, if you are purchasing another home once you sell your current one, you may want to ask for a discount on the second home inspection!**

lawsuit. An inspector can be found liable of having committed fraud if he or she does not have the credentials, is not trained in the way that he or she represents, or if an inspection was not actually conducted. Alternatively, an inspector can be held liable for gross-negligence if the inspection was conducted while he or she was intoxicated or under the influence of illegal narcotics or other substances.

Now that we have covered disclosure issues and inspections in depth, let's examine the second way a seller may be sued: premises liability.

CHAPTER SIX

❖

SELLER NIGHTMARE #2: PREMISES LIABILITY

Take a moment and imagine you are the homebuyer and no longer the seller. Envision that after months and months of seeking the perfect home for you and your family, finally, what *appears* to be the perfect property pops up on the market. You just know in your heart that a property like this won't be on the market for long. So you call your agent to make an appointment for that same day. You are overwhelmed with excitement!

Later that day, you show up to the property, all smiles. Your agent opens the door and you rush in to start touring what you feel will be your future home. But before you are able to even take three steps in, you immediately slip, fall, and fracture your wrist in three different places.

While there is no denying you were injured, the question becomes, *is the property owner liable for your injury?*

Often times, injured people assume that since they were hurt on someone else's property, the property owner is liable. However, this is not always true. And unfortunately, the law on this type of situation — also known as premises liability, which governs slip and fall type accidents — can be very complex since there is no cut-and-dry way to determine liability. In fact, the outcome for premises liability cases can drastically differ depending on the jurisdiction. In some states, the law is in favor of the owner while in others, it favors the injured. This is why knowing the law is essential, so that you can prevent a legal nightmare from being born. Generally, in Maryland, an injured Plaintiff bears the burden of proving many elements before liability is granted in their favor. As such, the law gives a bit of deference to the home or business owner in slip and fall cases.

Additionally, premises liability cases are situational, in that they are assessed based on their unique circumstances. In order for a property owner to be held responsible, the injured party would have to prove that the owner was liable through one of three elements, including:

1. That the property owner caused the unsafe or dangerous condition. This includes causing a liquid spill, a tear in the carpet, or by digging a hard-to-spot hole.
2. That the property owner knew about this condition, yet still did not improve or fix the condition so that any subsequent injuries could have been preventable.
3. That the property owner should have been aware about the condition because a "reasonable" person would have noticed the problem and taken steps to prevent injuries. Therefore, the owner has a duty to exercise reasonable care in the management of the property. If the owner breaches this duty, they may be liable due to negligence.

The majority of premises liability cases argue the third factor because all property owners have an innate duty to maintain a safe environment. Owners will often contend that they did not have actual knowledge of the defects. In these cases, the question becomes, did they have *constructive* knowledge, or in other words, *should* they have known. This does not mean that the property owner has a duty to repair all potential hazards and maintain a property in perfect shape. It does however mean that the property owner s*hould* provide some warning of any dangerous conditions that are not readily apparent. Additionally, it means that the property owner *should* act promptly to correct or remedy any dangerous conditions.

Be aware, though, that members of the public or invitees also have a duty to exercise reasonable care. Invitees are expected to notice obvious hazards and act reasonably in keeping away from them. Additionally, if an invitee engages in an inappropriate, careless, or negligent manner, the property owner may be absolved completely or at least partially of any liability, depending on the jurisdiction. For example, if you host an open house after having just mopped the floor (for the record, I would advise against mopping right before hosting an open house) and place a large yellow "CAUTION WET FLOOR" sign, you may not be found liable if the prospective buyer starts doing cartwheels on the floor.

In Maryland, we observe a contributory negligence standard, which makes it even more difficult for a victim to seek justice. Under this rule, if the injured party fails to exercise due care, which contributes to even 1% of the fault, then that injured party is 100% barred from recovering for any loss or injury.

In contrast, some states follow the comparative negligence standard, which states that if the injured party and the other party both contributed to the injury because they each failed to exercise due care, then the damages awarded to the injured party are decreased in direct proportion to his or her own negligence. To illustrate, if the injured party was doing cartwheels on a wet floor that had a large yellow sign stating "CAUTION WET FLOOR" when he fell and broke his leg, then the jury may find that he was comparatively negligent by 50% and thus, is only entitled to 50% of the entire damages amount. In other words, if the total amount awarded were $100,000, then they would only be entitled to $50,000.

TYPES OF PREMISES LIABILITY CASES

Clearly, in situations where you invite prospective buyers into your home, either through a private appointment or an open house, you owe them a duty to keep them reasonably safe. Let's take a closer look at the different types of premises liability cases and what a property owner such as yourself, can do to limit your liability.

The most common type of premises liability cases include slip-and-falls. Most slip (or trip) and fall accidents in residential real estate stairs, rugs/carpets/floor, or slipping due to ice or snow. Sometimes, stairs can be unsafe for individuals who are not accustomed to them the same way the home sellers are. The factors that can contribute to hazardous stairs include the steps being too steep, shallow, or of varying heights. Or, there could be a complete lack of or poorly designed handrails, lack of proper lighting, or an object on the stairs. These factors can result in negligence, but sometimes, an accident can occur because an individual is wearing a long dress or other garment, and trips on the cloth, in which case, the homeowner is clearly not at fault.

Another common contributor to slip-and-falls includes rugs, carpets, or the floor. If an area rug does not have the proper grip pad underneath it, it can be a serious hazard. Other hazards include carpets or rugs with holes in them, or with frayed edges. As previously discussed, floors can be slippery when they are freshly waxed or wet.

Ice and snow also give rise to homeowner's liability. Although homeowners have a duty to *reasonably* remove ice and snow and to make the sidewalks or paths *reasonably* safe, winning an ice or snow case in states that experience harsher cold weathers than others will not be easy. In other words, what is considered as *reasonable* in the State of Maine will be very different to the State of South Carolina. Further, jurors are often reluctant to find homeowners liable because they tend to feel that ice and snow are known hazards, which the invitee should expect.

While it is generally the municipality's job to repair public sidewalks, a homeowner must act reasonably to keep their internal walkways, driveways, and paths in reasonably safe conditions. Additionally, homeowners should make sure that there is adequate outdoor lighting. Therefore, it is important that property owners regularly examine and maintain the exterior of their home.

Finally, if you have a pet, it is always advisable to place the pet in the care of a relative, neighbor or pet-care service when the property is being shown to prospective buyers. This is because in some states, including Maryland, dog bites are considered a type of premises liability. In other words, landlords and owners are liable for the injuries to others caused by their pet — usually dogs. With this information, you should proceed with caution if you decide to allow your dog to roam free during a showing. At best, dogs are a distraction during an open house or private showing and at worst, they are a liability.

TAKE PREVENTATIVE ACTION

Sellers should take a proactive approach to minimizing the risks associated with premises liability. By doing so, you will not just reduce the likelihood of an accident occurring, but you will also be in a better position to demonstrate that you did your due diligence. Thus, if ever faced with a lawsuit, this will reduce your exposure to liability since your proactive approach will work to your benefit. Also, it goes without saying that both the seller and the real estate practitioner can be held liable, so make certain that your real estate agent is also aware of any potentially hazardous areas.

The first step that every home seller should take is to review their Homeowner's Liability insurance and make sure that they are covered in the event of a lawsuit during showings or open houses. Since even the most conscientious homeowner can find him or herself facing a lawsuit, liability coverage can help prevent the homeowner from having to pay out of pocket to defend a case. Some examples of protections that homeowner's liability coverage may provide include medical bills, lost wages (even future wages), pain and suffering, interest, and legal costs. Make sure you are clear what your insurance covers so that you don't experience any surprises later on.

Secondly, the homeowner should properly identify any potential hazards with a thorough inspection. In fact, while it may seem overly cautious, it's in the best interests of the homeowner to document the inspection and file it away in the event it is needed for a lawsuit defense. A simple move-in checklist that is typically used when tenants move into a property would be best, as they are detailed from room to room. Once you have done a thorough check, make sure you share your findings or even the document with your agent. This way, they can keep it in their records or better yet, they can pass along that information to the buyer agent when they are scheduling the showing who will then pass along the information to their buyer. Yet another proactive step you can take is to warn all guests, either verbally, through proper signage, or by blocking/taping off the hazardous areas.

Other proactive steps include removing all rugs (even those with rubber-backing and secured with tape) and clearing the staircase of books, magazines, shoes, or other decorative pieces, which would eliminate many of the sources of slips and trips. Also, think twice about using candles during open houses and showings, as this could be a major disaster. Alternatively, you may choose to leave a few lights on to create both a cozy environment while also providing sufficient lighting.

As you can see, there are certain liabilities that you are exposed to when you place your property on the market. However, your liabilities are not limited to the defects you disclose or to premises liabilities. Yet another way that sellers expose themselves to liability is through a less commonly known manner known as seller's remorse, which we will cover in the upcoming chapter.

CHAPTER SEVEN

❖

SELLER NIGHTMARE #3: SELLER'S REMORSE

Humans are incredibly interesting creatures. We like to think we always make sound and logical decisions, but this is not always the case. Sometimes, our decisions and behaviors are based on emotion and desperation, which we then try to justify through rationalization. Other times, our decisions are based on our gut instincts, sometimes the decision just *feels* right. We often don't need to justify decisions based on our instincts, because we trust our gut, even when our analytical understanding of a situation contradicts our instincts. Either way, regardless of how we come to make decisions, our decisions have an enormous influence over our lives.

Particularly, one specific decision is crucial in the sale of your home — the decision to sell. Deciding to sell is not something that should be taken lightly. Instead, a potential home seller should face all the facts and figures before listing their property on the market. When a home seller fails to take the time to think their decision through, they increase their probability of experiencing what we call seller's remorse, which comes with a list of its own costs and headaches.

DEFINING SELLER'S REMORSE

What is seller's remorse? Though less common than buyer's remorse, it is the feeling of regret over selling your home, which can be triggered by a multitude of reasons and circumstances. One of the main reasons sellers experience this phenomenon is because of price. On the one hand, a seller may not receive their asking price and thus, may believe they are accepting a low offer. On the other hand, when a prospective buyer quickly accepts the seller's counteroffer, the seller may begin to question whether they had priced their home too low in the first place. Either way, one of the main contributing factors to seller's remorse is often price.

Sellers may also feel remorse due to the emotional attachment that many people have towards their house. For many sellers, they do not view a house as merely an object, but instead, a home is where sweet memories were created — where holidays were spent gathered around with family and friends, where children grew up, or perhaps, where the seller grew up as a child. When a seller is faced with selling a home, they are faced with the harsh reality that they may never step foot in that home again. Thus, putting a home on the market may mean wrestling with the emotional heft of facing these realities.

Some of the other reasons why people develop seller's remorse include: impulsive decisions to list a home, the inability to find a home that is better or as good as the former home, a job opportunity that did not pan out as planned, change in financial situations for better or worse, altered family situations such as reconsidered divorces, or health issues that result in a miraculous recovery. Regardless of the reason, canceling a transaction is not easy and can potentially have costly consequences.

Before we explore the legal ramifications a seller may face, let's briefly explore how and when a buyer can refuse to move forward with a and what consequences they may face.

BUYER DEFAULTS

For the most part, Purchase Agreements place more control in the hands of a buyer than they do for a seller. This is because it is the buyers who are in control of the contingencies. For example, these contingencies include taking actions in a timely manner for property inspections, conducting appraisals, and getting financed within a certain time period. While a homebuyer is responsible for performing these tasks, these contingencies will also allow a buyer to cancel the transaction and still be entitled to having their full earnest money deposit returned to them.

For example, in regards to meeting the financing contingency, if the lender is not able to grant the loan, a buyer will not be forced to purchase the home. After all, a buyer can't buy a home that they can't afford. Further, a buyer will not be forced to purchase a home if the inspection reveals issues beyond that which the seller agrees to repair. In these situations, the buyer may also cancel the agreement and be entitled to the earnest money deposit. Therefore, if a buyer backs out of a contract under one of the several contingencies that affords them the right, then they can do so with no repercussion.

However, a buyer will not be able to keep the deposit if he or she backs out of the transaction when it is outside the scope or timeframe of a contingency. Under this scenario, the seller will typically be able to keep the deposit, sue to force the transaction to move forward, or can sue for damages. In these types of situations, it would be wise for a seller to proceed to try and sell the property to a third person, since doing so would mean that the seller is attempting to mitigate (or reduce) the amount of damages that they would have incurred from the loss of the sale. Mitigation of damages is something that the courts view favorably. Then, once the home has sold to a third party, the seller may file a lawsuit against the original buyer, assuming the price to the third person was less than the contract price of the initial buyer who backed out of the deal.

Another aspect of a buyer defaulting is the Liquidated Damages clause. A Liquidated Damages provision allows for the payment of specified damages when the buyer breaches the contract. The benefit of such a provision is that it saves the parties from spending time, money, and energy fighting over damages if the buyer defaults. Therefore, the parties are essentially waiving their right to sue if things go wrong. But in order for such a provision to be enforced, both parties must sign and acknowledge this provision. While on the surface, it may seem like a good idea for a seller to agree to this provision; this is not always the case.

When it comes to signing or initialing a liquidated damages clause, sellers must beware. This is especially true if the liquidated damages clause strictly refers to how the deposit is handled. In this circumstance, the seller needs to make sure that the amount of the deposit would be sufficient in covering any potential costs. For example, if the buyer gives a $1,000 deposit and decides to walk away from the transaction only two days before settlement, this $1,000 might be a mere drop in the bucket in comparison to what a seller's actual damages are.

At this point, the sellers may have already hired a moving truck, a moving company, have quit their jobs, packed, and have placed deposits on their new home. Clearly, $1,000 won't even remotely cover the costs already incurred, much less the costs a seller will continue to incur in order to resell to another buyer. As you can see, the Liquidated Damages Clause should always be closely examined and understood before signed.

While a buyer has several opportunities to back out of a contract, sellers have far fewer options afforded to them. A seller may think that he or she can just simply change his or her mind, but whether he or she does so lawfully should be a major consideration. If done unlawfully, the buyer may be entitled to legal remedies, which can be both costly and time-consuming.

Before we discuss the legal ramifications, let's explore the ways in which a seller may lawfully back out of a contract.

SELLER LAWFULLY DEFAULTS

It should be noted that the legal remedies available to a seller depends on where in the negotiation process the buyer and seller stand. For example, if the buyer tours the home and happens to run into the seller while he or she is present, and the buyer and seller discuss purchasing the property and "shake on it," no matter how hard they shake hands, or for how long they talk about it, the seller can lawfully decide to not sell, assuming nothing was in writing. You see, when it comes to the sale of real estate, regardless of which state you are located in, an oral agreement and a handshake are not strong enough to be upheld in a court of law. This is because, under the legal concept of the Statute of Frauds, any contract for the sale of land or property must be in writing in order to be enforceable. Therefore,

SELL YOUR HOME WITH CONFIDENCE

if there was no sign, sealed, and delivered Purchase Agreement, then the buyer will not have any legal justification to pursue a lawsuit against the seller.

Of course, such a situation can be incredibly frustrating for a prospective buyer who was depending on the word and integrity of the home seller. But the Statute of Frauds works to protect both the buyer and the seller — it's a two-way street. Think of it like this: although the buyer may be frustrated after a seller decides to break his or her word, a seller cannot force a buyer to move forward and purchase the home after having expressed only verbal interest.

While a seller may think it's all fun and games and decide to just not sell after a verbal agreement, they cannot do that after they have signed on the dotted line. Once the offer has been signed, it becomes a legally binding and enforceable contract. Therefore, if you decide you do not want to sell after having signed, I would advise that before you notify the buyers, review the Purchase Agreement first. Specifically, there are three areas to check.

First and foremost, check your contingencies and addendums. Specifically, if there was a stipulation stating that you must first find an adequate replacement home, then you may be able to refer to that as a legitimate reason for backing out of the contract. A seller may want to include such an addendum if he or she is concerned about not being able to find a suitable home to buy. This type of contingency gives a seller a period of time to locate another home without an obligation to sell to the buyer if a new home is not found.

Or, perhaps you need the approval of a family member, who has a financial interest in the sale of the home. If you incorporate this provision into your contract, it may be another way to back out of the agreement. Either way, you should always check your contract to see if it affords you a contractual and legitimate way out.

Additionally, if the buyer has missed one of his or her deadlines that were set in the contract, this could be yet another way a seller could lawfully cancel the agreement. Real estate contracts are full of deadlines and requirements for both the buyer and seller, but it is especially important for the buyer to meet them. For example, if a buyer was supposed to make an application for a loan within seven days of the ratified contract, but it's now been ten days, a seller may be able to cancel the contract without repercussions. Very commonly, I have seen buyers ask for a thirty or a forty-five day close and try to extend that time period. In a situation like this, a seller may decide not to extend any further and to cancel the contract.

Finally, a seller may be able to back out of a contract if an important signature is missing from the contract. In this type of scenario, it is usually the fault of the agent who fails to procure the necessary signatures. For instance, it is not uncommon for the buyer and seller to make a verbal agreement but then the agents fail to follow up with signatures. If this happens, the seller may be able to get out of the contract, depending on if the signature is vital to the agreement.

SELLER UNLAWFULLY DEFAULTS

If the seller is unable to find a lawful escape through the contingencies and deadlines within the Purchase Agreement, then the seller will have no choice but to breach the contract. Breaching the contract is a risky strategy, as it places the seller in a legally vulnerable position while it gives the buyer *several* options for recourse. This is why a seller is best advised to be absolutely firm about their desire in selling their property; sellers can face high hurdles when they decide to back out of a contract for the sale of property.

At best, the buyer may be empathetic to a seller's reason for breaching the contact. Ideally, the buyer may simply accept an apology and move on to the next property. At worst, the buyer will not be understanding and will take the seller's decision to not move forward with the sale as a showing of bad faith. This scenario typically tends to occur when the seller waits until he or she is nearing the closing date, and the buyer has invested large sums of time and money in ensuring that they are moving forward.

But like most things, money talks. If a seller finds themselves in this type of situation, a seller is wise to offer compensation to the buyer for their lost expenses, time, and perhaps more importantly, for the opportunity to have, quite possibly, purchased their dream home.

In deciding what amount a seller should offer, the sellers should weigh a few different factors. At first glance, a seller may be inclined to simply offer the buyer their earnest money deposit and call it a day. However, in most states, when a seller defaults, the buyers are entitled not just to the deposit, but also to an amount that will cover their direct damages. Direct damages are those expenses and costs that a reasonably, ordinary and prudent person would expect the non-breaching party to incur from a breach. Therefore, the seller should consider compensating the buyer for any and all expenses the buyer has incurred in relation to the purchase. Some examples of direct damages that the buyer may incur include inspections, surveys, and appraisals. However, if the case goes to court, the buyer might also sue to recover consequential damages, too.

CONSEQUENTIAL DAMAGES

If a buyer decides to pursue a lawsuit against a seller for their default, they will certainly sue for consequential damages in addition to the direct damages. Black's Law defines consequential damages, as "damages that that don't directly come as the result of an action but are a consequence of the action." As such, these types of losses go beyond the contract itself and into the actions that occurred due to the seller's failure to proceed with the sale. In the real estate world, a buyer can be greatly inconvenienced by a seller's decision to not move forward with the sale. In most cases, the consequential damages can include the cost of storage, lost deposits on moving arrangements, temporary housing, and living expenses. While these expenses could be enough to make any logical seller to balk, there are actually two other costly consequential damages that most sellers do not even consider.

The first costly form of consequential damages that home sellers often fail to recognize are commission payments to real estate agents, specifically, the buyer agent. Depending on the wording contained within a buyer-broker agreement, a buyer's agent could be entitled to commission once they have submitted an offer and it is approved. If there is language in the buyer-broker agreement stating that the buyer has to pay their agent a commission once an offer is accepted, the buyer may tack this cost into the suit against the seller. However, it should be noted that even though the agent may be legally entitled to their commission payment, rarely will a buyer agent enforce this term of the agreement. This is because it is in the best interest of the agent to maintain a positive relationship with their buyer client in hopes of continuing their working relationship with that client, After all, even though the transaction did not successfully close for this property, the buyer will likely still need to buy a property and therefore, the agent will want to still be used for that purchase.

As for the seller's own agent, keep in mind that you may also be liable to them, too. But since the fee paid to the listing agent is not considered a consequential damage that the buyer will ask for in a lawsuit, we will refrain from further discussing it in this section, but we will revisit this topic later in the chapter.

The second costly consequential damage that home sellers often fail to acknowledge are lost profits that the buyer may incur when the sale does not move forward. These types of situations are more often seen when the buyer is a real estate investor. In these situations, a seller can be found liable for potential profits that could have been made if the investor was planning on rehabbing and selling the property or, if they were planning on turning the property into a rental property.

All things considered, it is clear that the best option for many sellers is to just go ahead and offer an amount of compensation that is adequate for buyers to cover their expenses. If not, the seller may be faced with not just the costs associated to direct damages and consequential damages,
but also with legal fees, including the costs of the buyer's attorney, your own attorney, and court costs.

While these costs may seem like a bad dream, the real nightmare happens when and if the buyer attempts to force the sale under what is called a specific performance suit.

SPECIFIC PERFORMANCE

If the buyer feels that they cannot be made whole through monetary means, the next remedy they will seek is to force the seller to sell the property, regardless of the seller breaching the contract. This type of suit is called specific performance, which allows a court to not only order money damages, but to also order the seller to sell the property and convey title to the buyer according to the terms of the original contract.

This remedy is based on the premise that every piece of real estate is inherently unique because there is no other property that is built on that specific piece of land. And as such, the buyer cannot be made whole or remedied unless the seller moves forward with the purchase.

Generally, when a scorned buyer sues for specific performance, they will also file a *lis pendens* against the title of the property, while the case is being adjudicated. *Lis pendens* is Latin for "litigation pending," which places a lien on the property. Therefore, by filing a *lis pendens*, the buyer is effectively notifying other potential buyers that litigation is pending against the property, which renders the property unmarketable. When the property becomes unmarketable because of a *lis pendens*, this will ultimately place a cloud on title. When this happens, the seller will be unable to sell the home in the future until they have cleared the *lis pendens* by either following through with the deal with the original buyer or by reaching some other sort of financial settlement with the original buyer. This is because before a title company can issue title insurance to any buyers, the title needs to be clean and free of any encumbrances or liens.

Clearly, a spurned buyer can take a seller to task if the seller breaches the contract. However, the courts will also require the buyer to meet a high burden of proof in showing that he or she was in fact, a ready, willing, and able buyer. Sellers will want to point to any time the buyer attempted to renegotiate the contract to bolster the claim that the buyer did not have the intent of moving forward with the purchase. For example, if a buyer requests repairs or asks for further price reductions, a seller could argue that a buyer did not fully agree to the purchase, because the sale was still subject to negotiations. Under such circumstances, if the buyer meets his or her burden, the seller may end up not only being forced to sell the property, but also having to pay thousands of dollars in legal fees along the way. Therefore, the seller can expect to face some legal headaches if and when a monetary award cannot easily remedy the buyer.

CANCELLING THE LISTING AGREEMENT

As previously mentioned, when and if the seller prevents the Purchase Agreement from commencing, they have another agreement they will have to deal with: the listing agreement with their agent. When a seller stops the sale of their home, he or she is usually still on the hook for paying commission to an agent, because most Exclusive Right to Sell Agreements include a stipulation stating that the agent earns his or her commission when he or she procures a ready, willing, and able buyer, who purchases at the price that is accepted by the seller. At that point, the agent has spent time, effort, and money in advertising and marketing and has thus earned his or her paycheck.

However, in most markets, listing agents these days do not bind the seller to this stipulation if the seller changes his or her mind. After all, most agents depend on referrals for their business, and I am willing to bet that an agent who enforces this stipulation will greatly reduce their chances of having that seller ever refer them any future business. Nevertheless, if you do decide to hire an agent to sell your home, it would be wise for you to ask the agent what would happen if you were to decide to not move forward with a sale. At best, they allow you to cancel the listing with no issues. At worst, you may owe them for their marketing expenses *and* commission.

TIPS TO AVOID SELLER'S REMORSE

As you can see, the phenomenon of seller's remorse comes with its own set of unique considerations and challenges. Unfortunately, there is no easy way out for a seller after he or she has signed on that dotted line. Fortunately, a seller can manage the emotional rollercoaster of selling his or her home and reduce their chances of experiencing seller's remorse once the reality of the situation hits.

First off, a seller should re-examine his or her original pros and cons list for selling, including their physical, emotional, and financial reasons. When evaluating the benefits and drawbacks of selling, the seller should not forget to acknowledge the flaws of the home, such as being too small or too big and the location not being ideal. Sellers should ask themselves, "What's keeping me from moving on and closing this chapter?" and "What can I focus on in the future to help me get over the stress of leaving this home?" Very often, when sellers revisit this list, they find that the reasons for selling were quite compelling, especially after evaluating the costly consequences of potentially being sued.

Speaking of lawsuits, if and when you are faced with seller's remorse or a lawsuit, this is a good time to seek the professional services of an attorney to help clarify your available options. With this being said, I truly believe that in the absence of any extenuating situations, most attorneys will advise a seller to simply move forward with the sale. If this is the case, I would suggest you come to terms with your initial decision to sell, simply give yourself time to get accustomed to the change, and focus on the future.

CHAPTER EIGHT

❖

SELLER NIGHTMARE #4: VICARIOUS LIABILITY

Vicarious liability is a form of indirect liability that is imposed when two parties have a particular relationship where the superior is held responsible for the acts of a subordinate. One type of vicarious liability is *respondeat superior*, which is Latin for "let the master answer." *Respondeat superior* applies when an employer is held liable for an employee's negligent actions or omissions that occur during the course and scope of the employee's employment.

Thus, the doctrine of *respondeat superior* is a fixture of agency law that categorizes an employee as an agent for his or her employer, the principal. As such, the employer and the employee can be found jointly liable for the act that only the employee committed, and a plaintiff need not show that the employer was independently negligent, but must only prove an employment relationship existed. Therefore, the individual injured could proceed against the employee, employer, or both for payment of damages. This type of liability is deeply rooted in public policy, since an employer will generally be in a better financial position than his or her employees and therefore, the victim will be able to gain sufficient compensation.

How is this relevant to selling a home?

When a seller agrees to work with and hire an agent, they must sign a listing agreement with that agent, which enters him or her into an agency relationship. Now, before we move on to discussing how you can be held liable for the actions of your agent, it is important for you to be aware that there are in fact several different types of listing agreements. This may be surprising since usually, an agent will only present a seller with one type of agreement, commonly referred to as an exclusive right to sell. However, I believe it is important for you to understand the difference between the different types of listing agreements so you can decide which one is the best option for you.

Let's examine the different types of listings.

- **Exclusive Right To Sell Listing**. This is the most commonly used type of listing in which the listing agent has the most control. Under this type of instrument, regardless of whether the seller, the listing agent, or a cooperating buyer's agent finds a ready, willing and able buyer, the listing agent will earn a commission.
- **Exclusive Agency Listing**. Under this agreement, only one broker is employed to sell the property. However, the owner still retains the right to sell the property without compensating the listing broker. Due to the lack of control, most real estate agents are reluctant to work on an exclusive agency listing since they may do all the work only to have the seller find a buyer and exclude the agent out of the transaction.
- **Open Listing**. Similar to an exclusive agency listing, the owner retains the right to sell the property. The only other difference is that more than one broker is employed to sell the property, and only the broker who is able to procure a buyer whose offer the owner accepts, receives a commission. As you can imagine, this is not a popular type of listing arrangement, because few brokers would be willing to put in the work, only to have another broker bring in a buyer and claim the commission. Additionally, the owner is unrepresented and thus, the owner is only paying the buyer's agent's commission.
- **Net Listing**. Under this agreement, a seller lists his or her property for sale at a specified amount to one broker, and instead of earning a commission based on a set percentage, the broker retains the difference between the list price and the sale price. These types of listings are illegal in some states, so make sure to reference your state laws or consult with an attorney before

entering into this type of agreement. These types of agreements are dangerous, because if the agent obtains a purchase price far above the seller's listing price, the seller may accuse the listing agent of not disclosing the home's true market value. On the other hand, if the agent receives a low purchase offer close to the net price, the agent might be tempted to not present the offer to the seller if the agent finds that he or she will not be paid much.

- **Pocket Listing**. Finally, this type of listing is one that is not marketed on the Multiple Service Listing (MLS). Perhaps the property sells before the agent even has time to place it on the MLS or the homeowner chooses to go this route due to the level of privacy it affords them. This is especially common for public figures who don't want their address publicized. Additionally, even though it might limit the pool of buyers, the buyers who are interested are those who are willing to pay a premium for the ability to place an offer before it reaches the market.

Clearly, there are several different types of agreements that a seller can choose from. Typically, your agent will present you with just one option: the Exclusive Right To Sell Agreement. However, it is important for you to know that the terms within any listing agreement are 100% negotiable. Additionally, it may be beneficial to have an attorney explain the terms and revise them for you. Specifically, an attorney can also help you understand how and when the agreement terminates and if and when you become liable to pay a brokerage commission, even if a sale does not occur during the course of the agreement. An attorney can also draft an addendum specifying which items of personal property will be sold along with the house as well as which fixtures and appliances are specifically excluded. An attorney can also help you negotiate the best duration of the listing agreement based on your unique circumstances. The ways an attorney can help will be discussed at more length in Part Two.

Once a listing agreement has been signed, if you were to place the agent in a position that enables and causes your agent to commit either negligent or tortious acts to a buyer, then both you *and* your agent will be subject to liability. In other words, if tortious acts were performed through the duty created by the listing agreement, you and the agent could both be found liable and responsible for damages.

However, often times, a wronged buyer will have difficulty suing the seller - even if he or she was the main perpetrator. This is because often times, the seller has moved out of state lines or maybe out of the country, and cannot be readily located. Moreover, since an agent often makes a living from servicing the same clients, they are less likely to move from a particular area, so it is much easier to locate a real estate agent and thus, easier to sue the agent. Additionally, real estate professionals are seen as convenient deep pockets that appear to have the money to pay a claim, or they are otherwise insured for these types of predicaments. Either way, whether a seller can be easily located or not, it is important for you to understand what the law expects of real estate agents so that in turn, you are better informed as to what standards you should hold your agent against. As a result, this can ultimately lead to fewer lawsuits being filed by disgruntled buyers, which is the main purpose of this book.

Even though there is a lack of an agency relationship between a listing agent and the buyer, the courts are increasingly recognizing that legal protection must be afforded to the buyer. As such, most courts hold that a broker or agent will be liable for both an intentional and an innocent misrepresentation made to the purchaser of real property.

Now, let's examine the different causes of action that can be brought against an agent, specifically, intentional misrepresentation and negligent misrepresentation.

INTENTIONAL MISREPRESENTATION

When an agent or broker possesses the actual knowledge of any facts that materially impact the value or desirability of the property through direct knowledge or through indirect knowledge made known to them by the seller, the agent will also have an affirmative duty to disclose.

To better understand this, let's examine the elements for intentional misrepresentation. At common law, the elements are stated as the following:

1. defendant made a false representation,
2. with knowledge or belief that the representation was false or without a sufficient basis for making the representation,
3. the defendant intended to induce the plaintiff to act or refrain from acting on the representation,
4. the plaintiff justifiably relied on the representation, and
5. the plaintiff was damaged as a result of his reliance.

In order for a purchaser to succeed under this law, each of the five elements must be met. Moreover, a seller or agent cannot utilize the defense of *caveat emptor*, which is Latin for "let the buyer beware," for this type of action. *Caveat emptor* is used to convey the notion that the buyer alone is responsible for checking the quality and suitability of goods before a purchase is made, which is typically done by a licensed home inspector. However, as we discussed earlier, there are limitations as to what an inspector can uncover during a home inspection, which is the case for latent defects. Thus, the courts have refused to recognize the validity of the *caveat emptor* defense in cases where an agent knowingly makes a misrepresentation, or when he or she omits a material fact to a buyer.

Clearly then, the duty to disclose is easily met when the agent has actual knowledge of a defect. A more difficult standard is when the agent unintentionally misrepresents a material fact concerning the property when he or she is acting as a conduit of information. Or said differently, when the agent is merely relaying incorrect or incomplete information to a buyer that was provided to him or her by the seller. This type of misrepresentation is known as negligent misrepresentation.

NEGLIGENT MISREPRESENTATION

Typically, an agent receives information pertaining to a property from the seller and then the agent relays this information to potential buyers when the agent distributes it on the Multiple Listing Service (MLS). If this information is erroneous or incomplete, the agent could be held liable to the buyer for misrepresentation, when the information is either blatantly misleading or if the information partially suppresses or conceals information.

For a purchaser to meet the elements for this course of action, they must meet four out of the five elements for intentional misrepresentation as seen in the previous section. The only major difference is that the purchaser does not have to prove that the defendant made the misrepresentation with the intention to deceive nor do they have to prove that they had actual knowledge of the falsity of the statements. Instead, the agent will be found liable due to their failure to take proactive steps in ascertaining the facts themselves. This is why it is absolutely critical for agents to personally verify the information that is being provided to them concerning the property.

In order for an agent to show that they have indeed taken proactive steps to determine the accuracy of the information given to them by the seller, it is expected that the agent conduct a *reasonable* inspection of the property. A reasonable inspection is considered to have occurred when an agent walks through the premises and is able to personally examine the property. By doing so, the agent will be able to draw his or her own conclusions regarding the property and will be able to ascertain the degree to which the seller's representations were accurate and true. It is wise for a real estate agent to make a reasonable inspection of the property as part of their common practice, as it allows the broker/agent to protect himself or herself from liability due to the possibility of receiving inaccurate information from the seller.

For example, if a prospective purchaser is concerned with whether the property has sufficient parking spaces, the agent must not solely rely on the affirmation of the seller. The agent must make a visual inspection to determine the lot size or availability of the parking spaces. Moreover, an agent should inspect the property to discover any potentially hazardous conditions to warn prospective buyers who visit the property.

The question now becomes: *how broadly or narrowly should the agent's duty to investigate be defined?*

Depending on the jurisdiction, the courts apply a wide variety of standards in interpreting the agent's duty concerning the property. At one end of the spectrum, courts believe that agents have a duty to independently verify every single representation made by the seller. On the other end of the spectrum, some jurisdictions believe that agents should only have a duty to verify the representations made to them, when they have reason to believe they are false.

But due to the wide-ranging and unclear standard by which the courts can rule, understandably, the general public is confused about the duties owed to buyers. While the standard of behaving in a manner that is rooted in good faith and fair dealings is a solid starting point, it can be argued that from a public policy standpoint, buyers are owed an even stronger legal duty from a seller's agent. However, since an agent cannot be expected to know everything concerning real estate, courts should have more of a unanimous position that suggests that an agent would only be liable if he or she could have discovered the erroneous or missing information by exercising reasonable care. Then, if any material fact is found, it must be disclosed to the buyer who may choose whether or not to conduct a more extensive investigation. By holding this position, an agent's role would mandate more than that of a conduit of information between the seller and the buyer, in that they must take a more proactive approach.

Yet another way that home sellers may find themselves party to a lawsuit is through discrimination. While far less prevalent today than years before, discrimination continues to unfortunately be an issue that needs to be addressed in this book. Although some sellers may be exempt from anti-discrimination standards, it's important to be aware of how these laws could affect you. Read on to the next chapter for an explanation of housing discrimination, and to learn what is considered fair and what is not.

CHAPTER NINE

❖

SELLER NIGHTMARE #5: DISCRIMINATION

If you're selling a home, you need to be aware of housing discrimination laws. These laws are memorialized in many different forms through a series of federal and state laws. However, the main law that offers buyers and tenants protection against housing discrimination is referred to as the Fair Housing Act (FHA) (42 U.S.C. §3602). Although there are several key aspects of the Act that target renters, this chapter will focus on the rights given to buyers.

Before we proceed in our discussion about housing discrimination, it is important to note that there are exemptions within the FHA and they specifically address residential home sellers. As such, if you fit in the following exempt categories, this chapter may not apply to you.

EXEMPTIONS

The following are exemptions within the FHA that carve out categories of owners and sellers not subject to housing discrimination laws:

- Owners of single-family homes who own fewer than three units at the same time. To qualify, owners cannot sell more than one house in a two-year period. Furthermore, the owner of the property may not employ a broker, agent, or any other real estate professional in the sale of the property. In other words, the owner can only sell as a For Sale By Owner, because real estate professionals must adhere to the FHA.
- If an owner chooses to live in their unit (also known as, owner-occupied), and they own no more than four units at a time, they would be exempt from the FHA. This is known as the "Mrs.

Murphy" Exemption.
- If a property is intended specifically for senior citizens, housing can be restricted to families and people with children. To qualify for this exemption, a property's individual units must be either occupied only by people over the age of 62, or, no fewer than 80% of people can be age 55 or older. This is known as the "Housing for Older Persons" Exemption.
- If an owner operates their house as part of a religious organization, or as part of a private club with limited membership, they would also be exempt from the FHA.

It is important to note that even if you're exempt from the FHA, it is illegal to discriminate when advertising the sale, rental, or availability of your house.

DISCRIMINATION IN ADVERTISING

When listing or otherwise advertising a home, a seller may not make preferential statements that limit the access of buyers from a protected category, or request specific buyer standards that may restrict people of a protected category. Further, a seller may not advertise the availability of a property, but then falsely deny the availability to another individual.

Under the FHA, the United States Department of Housing and Urban Development (HUD) specifically defines what is considered discriminatory when advertising a property. Specifically, the FHA identifies the words, phrases, and materials that should not be used. It would be wise to review this document to have some general knowledge of discrimination when advertising a property, which can be found at https://www.hud.gov/sites/documents/DOC_7781.PDF

After understanding the exemptions and how different words and phrases can make an advertisement discriminatory, it is important to understand how housing discrimination is defined under the FHA.

HOUSING DISCRIMINATION UNDER FHA

Housing discrimination occurs when an individual or a family is denied access to a home (through a sale or rental) because of a certain identity. A buyer applicant cannot be treated unfairly based on many different characteristics. Namely, the FHA has included the following "protected categories": race or color; religion; national origin; familial status or age (includes families with children under the age of 18 and pregnant women); disability or handicap, or sex.

"Familial status" and "families with children" can be a parent, a pregnant individual, or any person who has or is in the process of receiving legal custody over one or more individuals who are under the age of eighteen. Further, "disability or handicap" is defined within the FHA as any physical or mental "impairment which substantially limits one or more of such person's major life activities, a record of having such an impairment, or, being regarded as having such an impairment, but such term does not include current, illegal use of or addiction to a controlled substance."

HOUSING DISCRIMINATION UNDER STATE LAW

Fortunately for some buyers, many state laws give even *more* protection to homebuyers than the federal law under the FHA. As such, many state laws include even more "protected categories" that aren't covered by federal law.

For example, under Maryland law, Annotated Code of Maryland, State Government Article, Section 20-704, a buyer cannot be discriminated against under the three additional protected categories of marital status, gender identification, or sexual orientation. However, it is equally important to note when the rule will *not* apply with respect to discrimination on the basis of those categories. Under Maryland law, the exemption is granted when dealing with a rental of rooms within one home, when the owner resides in one of the rooms as a principal residence. Further, the rule does not apply when dealing with the rental of any apartment in a multi-unit building that contains no more than five rental units, if the owner maintains one of the units as his or her principal residence.

ENFORCEMENT PENALTIES FOR VIOLATIONS

The law provides several methods of enforcement when someone suspects they have been discriminated against. Namely, according to the Fair Housing Act, the options include filing an administrative complaint, a private lawsuit, or both provided that an Administrative Law Judge has not yet begun a hearing. For an administrative complaint, a person who believes that they have been (or even will be) a victim of housing discrimination may file a written complaint directly with the U.S. Department of Housing and Urban Development (HUD). The statute of limitations is one year after the discriminatory act occurred. According to the Fair Housing Act (FHA) (42 U.S.C. §3612), an Administrative Law Judge who finds that a respondent has committed a discriminatory housing act may impose a civil penalty of up to $10,000 for a first offense, up to $25,000 for a second offense within a five-year period, and up to $50,000 for a third offense within a seven-year period.

For a private lawsuit, the aggrieved person may file a civil action in the United States District Court or State Court within two years after the discriminatory act occurred or ended, or after a conciliation agreement was breached, whichever occurs last. Under this scenario, a federal judge may grant whatever relief is appropriate in order to vindicate the public interest, which may include an amount of up to $50,000 for the first violation and up to $100,000 for any subsequent violation.

Clearly, a person's status to buy a home should not be affected by factors that do not directly correlate with his or her eligibility to be a good buyer. However, sellers can still deny potential buyers for legal reasons such as having insufficient levels or proof of income, low credit scores, and poor financial history. Either way, it is important as a home seller to have some knowledge regarding housing discrimination, even if the laws do not apply to you in the sale of your current home.

CHAPTER TEN

❖

SELLER NIGHTMARE #6:
UNABLE TO ATTEND SETTLEMENT

Now that we have discussed all the ways in which a seller could potentially find him or herself party to a lawsuit, it is important to smoothly end the transaction in order to avoid potential headaches and expenses. Typically, a transaction will come to a close with the sellers, buyers, real estate agents and sometimes, lenders, all gathering at a big table where they sign the papers together. But other times, it does not work out this way. Instead, life may get in the way and throw a wrench in your ability to attend settlement.

Sometimes, these situations can arise last minute while others times, you may be aware of your inability to attend settlement long before the settlement date. Some examples of when settlement does not go as planned and prevents the parties from attending closing include illnesses, last minute trips, pregnancy due dates, simply moving to a different state or country, or even death. Either way, you should know that without a clear plan, you could end up exposing yourself and your heirs to unnecessary headaches and expenses. Therefore, you will want to immediately notify the buyers and the title company as to whether or not you will be able to attend settlement so that alternate arrangements can be made. Otherwise, you may face costly expenses if and when you miss the settlement date due to your lack foresight.

Upon notifying the title company of your inability to attend settlement, depending on the laws of your state and the unique circumstances to your transaction, the title company will provide you with a few different options. The first option is commonly referred to as a "Witness Closing" in which the title company coordinates a time and place with a notary public who will meet with you pre-sign the documents. When you decide to do a Witness Closing, you should note that there are some documents that need to be signed on the day of settlement. One document that needs to be signed on the day of settlement is the final settlement sheet, also commonly referred to as the Closing Disclosure (CD). The CD is a one to two page document that clearly breaks down of all the closing costs you are responsible to pay as well as what your net proceeds will be.

As such, whenever you pre-sign, you will likely authorize your real estate agent or attorney, through a very Limited Power of Attorney (POA), the ability to sign the final settlement sheet on the day of closing. We will discuss POA Agreements in more detail in just a moment, but if you are completely unfamiliar with POA Agreements, I highly recommend watching my free video mini course. You can visit, www.sellyourhomewithconfidencebook.com/course to learn more.

A second option that a title company may present you with is commonly referred to as a "Mail Away Closing." Under this option, if you are out of town and unable to pre-sign the documents, then the title company can mail all the documents directly to you. Then, you will be responsible for signing them in front of a Notary Public and sending the packet of documents back to the title company. Additionally, you will want to ship the documents back to the title company with ample time for them to review the documents to confirm that they were signed accurately and completely. This is why I do not suggest that you wait to the last minute because if there are any issues with your signatures, you will need to re-sign the documents which may cause delays tothe settlement date. And if settlement is delayed, it may cause the buyers to incur additional expenses such as rescheduling movers, additional payment of rent, and sometimes, even hotel expenses. You should also note that since these are expenses that were incurred by the buyer because of delays caused by you, they might rightfully seek to have you cover these expenses. This is why it is so critical to have a clear course of action about what will happen if you are unable to attend settlement, so that there are no unexpected last minute delays.

Further, since it not uncommon for a seller to have an unexpected situation arise that prevents them from attending settlement, *I believe that it is absolutely critical for every seller to draft and sign a Power of Attorney (POA) as soon as they make the decision to sell.* In fact, drafting and signing a Limited POA Agreement is the final option that the title company will explore with you if you are unable to attend settlement. At its most basic level, a POA Agreement gives one person, commonly referred to as the agent, the power to act on behalf of another person, referred to as the principal. Power of Attorney Agreements are routinely used in real estate in that they allow your appointed agent (who is not to be confused with your real estate *agent*) to attend settlement on your behalf in order to sign all the necessary documents to close the transaction.

Often, home sellers will ask their significant others, friends, relatives or other trusted people to act as their agent. But regardless of whom you decide to appoint, you should absolutely educate yourself about all the ways that your agent can misuse his or her power. This is important since Power of Attorney Agreements are commonly referred to as "licenses to steal." However, by informing yourself from the onset about all the ways you could be mistreated through the use of the POA, you will have the necessary knowledge in order to take proper measures to prevent or mitigate your chances of experiencing abuse. Obviously, this is an incredibly important topic to understand, which is why I have included an entire video lesson about this in my mini course!

Finally, by having the forethought to create a POA *before* the need for one arises can save everyone significant time, effort, and money. By having a POA Agreement on your side, your real estate transaction can remain safeguarded and you can rest assured that settlement will move forward smoothly and successfully, regardless of whether or not any unexpected last minute situations arise.

Now, if and when you decide to use a POA Agreement for your settlement, there are several key elements to bear in mind. First and foremost, you should know that an agent cannot simply transfer their responsibilities under the POA to another person if they are unable to act. For example, if you nominate your daughter as your agent and she becomes ill on the day of settlement, she cannot transfer her rights to another person. This is why instead of naming just one agent, you will want to name alternate agents and/or successor agents in your agreement so that you can rest assured that someone, who you trust, will be able to step in if the original agent is unable to act or perform.

Additionally, you should note that most courts require that the original POA Agreement be attached and recorded along with the deed. As such, if a POA Agreement is used, you will need to give the original POA Agreement to the title company *long before* settlement so that they can confirm that it is in fact an enforceable and valid POA. The last thing you will want to deal with is handing the POA to the title company and them not recognizing the POA as a valid and legally enforceable document, which can happen for a multitude of reasons.

If the title company fails to recognize the POA as valid and you become incapacitated, you will not be able to simply draft and sign a new POA Agreement. This is because in order for a POA to be considered valid in the eyes of the court, the principal (the seller) must have signed the document *before* they became incapacitated. Therefore, if you become incapacitated and have signed an invalid POA, you will be unable to create a new Power of Attorney since you now lack the capacity to sign a legally enforceable Power of Attorney. As such, your appointed agent will be unable to sign on your behalf and finalize the sale. When this happens, since there is no one authorized to sign on behalf of the seller, the buyers may have no choice but to proceed with a lawsuit to force the sale, also known as specific performance. This is why it is so important to make sure that you are using a POA form that is valid and accepted by the title company.

But unfortunately, it has become fairly common for unsuspecting sellers and individuals to create POA Agreements that are invalid and thus, unenforceable. This is due to the fact that individuals are increasingly using fill-in-the-blank templates that are found online, which often fail to include statutorily required language specific to the state in which the property is located. And since it is difficult for a layperson with no legal training to decipher whether a form is truly valid versus it merely looking like it is valid, it would be wise for you to stay away from fill-in-the-blank templates. If you would like to learn more about this, be sure to refer to my mini-course where I further discuss issues relating to fill-in-the-blank templates in much more detail so you know what to watch out for.

Lastly, you should note that the validity of a POA Agreement dies along with the principal of the POA Agreement. As such, an agent can no longer sign on behalf of the principal once the principal dies. Upon the death of the principal, the POA loses its validity and instead, an executor or personal representative of the deceased seller must be appointed. Speaking of death, whether you decide to use a Witness Closing, a Mail Away Closing, or a Power of Attorney, the common thread between all these options is that they are only afforded to a seller who is still alive.

Now you may be thinking, *so what happens to the transaction if the seller dies before settlement but after signing a Purchase Agreement?*

Mistakenly, many people assume that the deal also dies along with the death of the seller. However, if a seller passes after the signing of a Purchase Agreement but before settlement, the estate of the seller must continue forward with the sale of the property. There are several different reasons to explain this. First and foremost, the contract will remain on foot since there is often language included in the Purchase Agreement that binds the deceased owner's heirs and successors to the terms of the Agreement.

But also, a real estate Purchase Agreement is considered to be an executory contract. Meaning, although a contract has been formed, an obligation or promise that was contained within the contract has yet to have been fulfilled by one or both parties. As such, when a seller signs a contract, they are expected to fulfill their requirement of signing the required paper work to officiate the sale at settlement. Therefore, when the seller is unable to sign, the Personal Representative of the estate will need to sign on behalf of the seller, which can be a lengthy process.

In most cases, a buyer will be empathetic to the situation of the sellers but will want to still proceed with the purchase. In this case, the manner in which the transaction moves forward will depend on several factors. Firstly, please keep in mind that the process will vary by state. Secondly, it will also be important to note whether the seller was a sole owner or if he or she owned the property with another person(s).

If there were co-owners, it will be important to note whether they held title as joint tenants with rights of survivorship or if they were tenants in common. If they held title as the former, then the surviving owner(s) automatically becomes the full owner(s) and as such, there shouldn't be any delays with settlement. In this situation, the living owner(s) will need to provide the title company with the Death Certificate at the time of settlement to prove that one of the owners passed away. The Death Certificate is then recorded along with the deed in the Land Records of the county clerk.

However, if the property was titled as tenants in common with no automatic rights of survivorship, then the estate will be probated. The estate will also be probated if the owner was a sole owner. Opening probate will mean that the court will need to appoint a Personal Representative who will have the authority to sign the settlement documents on behalf of the estate in order to complete the sale. But as mentioned earlier, the process is not always quick or smooth and a delay with the probate process may have adverse consequences for a buyer. This is especially true if the buyer were in a situation where they had sold their house, but were unable to simultaneously complete the purchase on your home. In this circumstance, the buyer could be entitled to damages that would be payable by the Personal Representative of the sellers' estate. Alternatively, in an effort for your estate to avoid having to pay damages, the Personal Representative may want to consider allowing the buyer to move into the home under a Pre-Settlement Occupancy Agreement. A Pre-Settlement Occupancy Agreement would mean that the buyer would move in and pay a pre-determined amount of rent until the probate process is complete and then, they would be able to proceed with the sale.

Also, speaking of missing settlement dates, if the buyer decides that they either do not want to wait around for the probate process to be completed or if they feel uncomfortable moving into a home where the seller may or may not have just died in, a buyer can lawfully get out of the contract. This is because just about every Purchase Agreement has strict deadlines that must be adhered to by all parties. And since the death of the seller will result in a lengthy probate administration, it may be impossible for those deadlines to be met. Therefore, this would allow the buyer to turn to the missed deadlines as a basis for backing out of the deal and having their deposit returned to them. As such, it would be wise for a seller who is terminally ill and who believes that they might pass before settlement to include a provision in the Purchase Agreement to allow for an automatic extension for any deadlines. This way, the buyer will not be able to simply walk away from the transaction, if the seller were to pass while they were still under contract.

As you can see, the sale of your property can still move forward if you were to pass away. However, these types of situations can become problematic if and when the heirs of your estate were expecting to inherit the home. If there were expectations, they might attempt to fight the sale. In this scenario, the heirs may want to simply return the buyers' earnest money deposit and to perhaps give an additional sum of money to cover any expenses that were incurred by the buyer. However, since every piece of real estate is viewed as unique from the eyes of the courts, money does not always sufficiently remedy a buyer. Therefore, the buyers can take legal steps to force the sale.

In order to force the sale, the buyers can file a lawsuit seeking the seller's estate to proceed with the sale under specific performance. Under specific performance, the estate will be forced to proceed with the terms of the contract. Therefore, in order to avoid any unnecessary complications, it may be worth having a discussion with your heirs, at the time you decide to sell your home, to explain to them that they can not and should not try to stop the sale in the event that you were to pass away. You may even decide to have this conversation with your heirs and loved ones at the time when you sign your Power of Attorney Agreement.

Now, the discussion of death may have you wondering, *what happens to the sale if the buyer dies?*

Similarly, if the buyer were to pass away before settlement, the Purchase Agreement will still remain valid. Although in the real world, most sellers will probably not force the sale and will instead just place the property back on the market. You should also note that although you could try to fight to keep the earnest money deposit, your efforts might prove futile, especially if the Purchase Agreement contained a financing contingency. If the Purchase Agreement contained a financing contingency, then it will mean that the buyer can back out of the contract if they are unable to secure a loan. And since a lending institution would be hard pressed to approve a loan for a dead buyer, the buyers' estate will be entitled to the earnest money deposit.

As you can see, the sale of your property will require you to pay close attention to the settlement date in order to mitigate any of the aforementioned stressful scenarios. Just a little foresight and action on your part can help ensure that you will have a successful and smooth settlement. But regardless of whether or not the need for the POA ever arises, a POA is an incredibly important document that every home seller should have. Again, this is why I highly recommend drafting and signing a Power of Attorney Agreement as soon as you make the decision to sell. In fact, I always tell my clients that a POA is even more important than a will. This is because a POA addresses the issues of maintaining and protecting your assets while you are still alive while a will is only concerned with how your assets will be divided once you are no longer around.

This is why every home seller should have a POA drafted. Or, at a minimum, you should have a discussion with your heirs about the fact that they should not fight the sale in the event of you passing away. By doing so, it will prevent a lot of unnecessary stress for everyone involved.

Now that we are clear about what happens in the event that you are unable to attend settlement, let's wrap up Part One of this book with a look at what happens if you were faced with litigation.

CHAPTER ELEVEN

❖

WHAT HAPPENS WHEN FACED WITH LITIGATION?

Because of the large amount of money involved in real estate transactions, today's market has unfortunately turned into a legal battlefield where both buyers and sellers are bringing actions at record rates. One reason for this increase in litigation is because real estate transactions have become increasingly complex. While the Purchase Agreement was once a simple two or three page document, it has now turned into a more than forty-paged document with multifaceted terms and conditions.

Additionally, there are now more real estate investors than ever before that are active in today's vibrant market. But since these investors often seek alternative types of financing or turn to creative methods to make a deal work, there is an increased likelihood that something will go amiss that will end in a lawsuit.

Another reason why there is an influx of lawsuits in real estate is that the state, federal, and even local jurisdictions are passing more and more laws that are expanding the duties and responsibilities of sellers and real estate professionals. For example, federal law now requires sellers and practitioners to disclose information regarding lead-based paint hazards. On a more local level, as of October 1, 2016, Montgomery County, Maryland law now requires that a single-family home located in the county must be tested for radon before completing a sale of the home. Therefore, it follows that when more and more laws are passed, and more duties are assigned to different parties involved in the transaction, there is a greater possibility that somewhere along the line, a mistake will be made.

However, by learning about the different ways that a potential suit may be made, more lawsuits may be avoided.

Now, assuming the buyer feels maltreated by the seller or his or her agent, a seller may then be faced with the expense and hassle of going to court. However, most Purchase Agreements include a clause that states, before a party may turn to the legal system for justice, they must first attempt to resolve their issues through what is called alternative dispute resolution (ADR). By requiring ADR, such as mediation, as a prerequisite to litigation, both parties may save tens of thousands of dollars in litigation and avoid unnecessary stress.

ALTERNATIVE DISPUTE RESOLUTION

An ADR clause stipulates that both the buyer and seller must first attempt to resolve a dispute or claim with the help of a neutral third party mediator. The Purchase Agreement will usually dictate who will be appointed as the mediator. Typically, The National Association of REALTORS® (NAR) will appoint a retired judge or attorney, who is authorized and certified to facilitate a resolution. A large distinction between having the issue resolved through mediation versus in a court is that a mediator's recommendations are not binding, unlike a court ruling. However, in my experience, since the appointed mediator is usually very experienced with real estate litigation, their recommendations often run parallel with how a court of law would view the claim. Therefore, a mediator's recommendations should be strongly considered before either party decides to move forward with litigation.

If either party is dissatisfied with the recommendations of the mediator, they can then turn to the courts to find a proper resolution. Once the Judge or jury has heard the case, if the court finds in favor of the buyer, the seller may be responsible for the costs of repairs, or any other damages that are a result of that claim.

For example, if the claim is for failure of the seller to properly disclose a defect, the court will determine damages through an analysis of the difference between the price paid for the property and the actual value of the property with the undisclosed defects. In order to determine this amount, the Judge or jury will first determine the actual value of the home based on market value through the testimony of an expert, such as an appraiser. Then, they will take this amount and subtract it by the amount paid for the property. This difference will then be recognized as the amount that the buyers overpaid for the property, which will be used as the basis for the amount to be awarded to the buyer. Furthermore, if the Judge or jury finds that the buyer cannot be adequately compensated through a monetary award, the buyer may be able to cancel or rescind the purchase, and possibly recover punitive damages, attorney's fees, and court costs, as provided within the contract.

In most situations, buyers and sellers agree to the recommendations of the mediator. However, if you or the other party decides to pursue litigation, there are several key factors to keep in mind. The first factor to bear in mind is what is known as Statute of Limitations.

STATUTE OF LIMITATIONS

Statutes of Limitation is a critical feature in the legal landscape as it places a limit to the length of time a party has to sue someone after a specified event has occurred that entitles a suing party to initiate a legal proceeding. However, once that specific period of time passes, the suing party is barred from filing a case. Each state has specific laws regarding the time frame for filing a lawsuit, but generally, the clock begins from the date the problem is discovered, or reasonably should have been discovered, or from the date the property was purchased.

Courts firmly uphold the statute of limitations because it promotes justice and public policy by preventing a claimant from bringing a stale case when evidence has deteriorated, witnesses have disappeared or moved away, and memories no longer recollect accurate facts. As such, it is important to note key dates since a defendant may be able to immediately dismiss a claim when the Statute of Limitations has passed.

PROPER DOCUMENTATION

Along with the importance of noting key dates, it is important for you to maintain records of all documents pertaining to the real estate transaction. These documents include invoices that were prepared by contractors for work completed on a home before it was placed on the market, as well as work completed that was requested by the buyer after the home inspection. By maintaining these documents, invoices will be readily accessible to reference, and evidence will be available to illustrate that repairs were made, which can help defend against an action brought at a later date.

Also, be sure to maintain files that include not only the Purchase Agreement, but also all addendums, disclosures, and disclaimers that were created by your agents and/or attorneys. It is also prudent to keep a copy of the settlement sheet. This is because, sometimes, sellers give credits on the day of settlement that can show that the certain funds were to be used towards a repair, in which case, the buyer could be prevented from seeking additional funds later on.

Home sellers should also make a habit of putting all statements in writing through email instead of making phone calls, because these correspondences are more readily available to be referenced in the future. If an organized file on these email correspondences is not maintained, the opposing party might make assertions that are inaccurate or incomplete, and there will be insufficient proof to verify those statements. Additionally, by using emails for all correspondence, the likelihood of a misunderstanding will be reduced, as each party will be able to refer back to the email for clarification or reminders about what was written.

FINAL THOUGHTS

Imagine receiving a letter in the mail from a local law firm, stating that the firm's client, the buyer for your home, wants to sue you. Your blood begins to boil as you think, "How dare they!" But after the initial shock and anger wear off, the next logical thought should be, "Can I afford to fight this?"

At the end of the day, lawsuits are expensive — as the saying goes: "The only people who win lawsuits are the lawyers, as they line their pockets." Unfortunately, all too often, home sellers end up paying an attorney so much money through fighting a lawsuit that winning the lawsuit hardly feels like a win. As such, it is my school of thought that unless the stakes are high, meaning $20k or more, settlement outside of court is the way to go.

On a final note, I believe that the best way to avoid litigation is to foster a good relationship between you and the buyer from the onset, as no one wants to sue someone they like. This is why I believe it is imperative to hire an agent or an attorney to allow them to handle the negotiations. By doing so, you allow them to handle the brunt of the work while allowing you to remain shielded.

Now, in Part Two, we will dive into the benefits of having a professional guide you through the process as we explore the differences between hiring an attorney versus an agent. We will also explore the role that a title company plays within the transaction. And finally, we will uncover some "secrets" within the real estate industry that you should be aware of as you decide which professional you want to hire to help represent your interests.

PART TWO:

CHOOSING
THE RIGHT
PROFESSIONAL

CHAPTER TWELVE

❖

BENEFITS OF HAVING A
PROFESSIONAL BY YOUR SIDE

Most of the time, two parties cannot reasonably come together in a transaction without the help of a neutral and knowledgeable party who can successfully facilitate and advise their respective client. This is true of all types of brokers, whether it be real estate, mortgage, stock, or any other field. Of course, the dynamics and reasons as to why there is a need for the broker differ between the various fields.

Regardless of whether you choose to hire a professional to represent you, or if you choose to sell a house on your own, you should understand why real estate professionals are in the mix in the first place. The reasons are threefold. Real estate professionals are beneficial for their negotiation skills, for properly marketing the property, and finally, for helping the home seller stay clear of any major pitfalls.

NEGOTIATION SKILLS

First and foremost, negotiation is an art that has to be learned, and in most cases, real estate professionals have a significant amount of experience dealing with negotiations - first negotiating with you to get hired, and then negotiating with the buyer's agent on your behalf.

"Limited Authority" is a negotiation tactic that is particularly helpful when using a professional in a real estate transaction. This method works well because the professional can buy time to further consider any counteroffers or unexpected requests by telling the prospective buyer that the professional must approve any request with an unseen higher authority, such as the homeowner. For example, if the buyer's agent states to your agent that they are requesting a $5,000 credit for a roofing repair, then the agent will say, "I need to run this by the homeowner." Alternatively, if you decide not to work with an agent and you are the sole owner, more likely than not, you will be the ultimate decision maker and therefore, you will not be able to use the limited authority tactic, unless you create a phantom person.

Another way that a professional can be helpful in the negotiation process is by getting a buyer to see beyond dollars and cents. Sometimes, a buyer's agent does not accurately advise his or her client of a home's true value. For this reason, a listing agent can craft a custom message to interested buyers reemphasizing the features, benefits, and upgrades, and thus, proving that a home is worth the asking price. This strategy often reignites the fire in the buyer by getting them to see how they will also win by accepting a seller's counteroffer and moving into their dream home. A proper understanding of the facts helps the buyer to move forward with the *home* that they want but at the *price* the seller wants. And again, this strategy is best used when a neutral party (your agent) can highlight the features.

Additionally, we often forget that real estate negotiations involve people with emotions. When the stakes are high, emotions can run extremely high, and during the sale of a home, emotions are heavily involved. Understandably, home sellers are emotionally tied to their home, as it can be a place where beautiful memories were made, which inflates the real value of the home. As a result, when a home seller over inflates the value of their home, they have ultimately done what is considered the kiss of death for a home sale. This is because the longer the property stays on the market; the more prospective buyers negatively view the property. However, since the professional is not emotionally attached to the item being negotiated, they are able to not only price the property competitively and accurately, but they can also negotiate with a cool head, which always leads to a better outcome and higher net proceeds for the seller.

PROPERLY MARKETING AND PRICING

Needless to say, an attorney will not handle the marketing aspects of a home sale. But properly marketing the property is where the expertise of an agent can be greatly beneficial, and it can be the driving force of why an agent is often preferred over an attorney.

Marketing is a crucial aspect of selling a home. After all, if there is the perfect buyer out there who is willing to pay full asking price for a home, if they never know about the home due to it not being properly marketed to the public, then you will never see that full asking offer. The most successful real estate agents are incredible marketers as they first need to know how to market to attract clients such as yourself, but more importantly, they need to know the latest tricks and tools in marketing the property.

Agents have systems in place that allow them to effectively and efficiently price and market homes to ready, willing, and able buyers. With strong pricing and marketing systems, an agent can position your property on the market to be incredibly compelling compared to the competition. In turn, this can help the property sell faster and for the highest price possible.

In fact, the area in which most For Sale By Owners (FSBO) fail is in the area of pricing and marketing. For this reason, be sure to head to http://bit.ly/sellwithconfidencebook and look at the free book that you can download, *Sell Your Home With Confidence: FSBO Edition*, which outlines exactly how you can properly price and market your property, if you choose to go the FSBO route!

HELP AVOID PITFALLS

It is important to hire someone who is familiar with potential pitfalls. The real estate process is terribly complex, and it is riddled with landmines that blow up indiscriminately, often years after a sale. This is why it is against the law to hire someone who is not either an attorney or a licensed real estate agent. Real estate professionals, both attorneys and agent help protect their clients, and keep them from becoming victims of the pitfalls associated to the real estate transaction.

These pitfalls are not just some scare tactic I'm throwing out there. After all, it's not like you're selling a sweater; a house is regulated by tons of state and federal laws. If any of these laws are violated, someone can easily sue you and win, and it will likely cost you far more than the couple of thousands of dollars that you are trying to save by doing it yourself.

What are these pitfalls? We discussed them in Part One of this book so if you need a refresher, be sure to re-read or skim that section, especially if you decide to forgo the use of a real estate professional. However, since real estate professionals are expected to know and abide by all laws, they can take a lot of the pressure off of you from having to internalize all of the material covered in Part One.

These are just a few examples of how having a professional intermediary can be beneficial. By having a real estate professional by your side, they can shoulder the responsibilities that many home sellers have neither the skill, patience, fortitude, or desire to take on. Also, by having a real estate professional in your corner, the only thing left for you to do is to educate yourself on how to conduct a thorough interview. The interview process is one that should not be taken lightly, which is why the next few chapters will focus on comparisons between expert professionals, who are well equipped to handle pitfalls, versus a novice.

Specifically, we will first explore the difference between all the different titles of real estate agents and what they mean. Then, we will discuss the duties that are owed to you by your professional. Then, we will dive into how you can identify a true professional. Finally, we will discuss the role of an attorney and a title company within your real estate transaction.

CHAPTER THIRTEEN

❖

WHAT'S IN A NAME?

In the world of real estate, there are many terms and phrases used that can be incredibly confusing to anyone who is not entrenched in the industry. For most sellers, this confusion begins with the dizzying array of titles available to describe real estate professionals. And before the sellers can pack their bags and boxes, they need to know exactly who they are dealing with and what duties are owed to them in order to make the most educated decisions regarding something as important as selling their property.

As discussed earlier, the real estate industry suffers from information overload, and one aspect of this concept can be seen with the overwhelming complexity of titles. In fact, I will be the first to admit that before I entered the real estate industry, it seemed that the jargon thrown around to describe the real estate professionals was purposefully made to be confusing. I was very unclear about the difference between a broker, an associate broker, a real estate agent, and a REALTOR®.

While I soon learned the differences, in my discussions with my own clients, it's clear that there is a lot of confusion among consumers, and rightfully so! Perhaps the obfuscating of titles are meant to mask the true responsibilities and duties assigned to each title, which in turn allows the professional to be less inclined to uphold the standards associated with that title. Or perhaps, the reason for the different titles was actually intended to make it as clear as possible to the consumer that each person with a different title has varying duties and degrees of responsibilities. Either way, when a seller is faced with the task of choosing between professionals with varying titles, they *should* understand the distinguishing characteristics and responsibilities of the titles in order to make more informed decisions. And only when sellers acknowledge these differences will the real estate industry become less obscure with the fog of half-truths, omissions, and outright prevarication.

In order to cut through this fog and gain a more accurate view of the real estate professional, it's helpful to start by understanding the differences between each of the titles. In this chapter, we will shed some light on the fundamental differences between the different titles and aim to clear up the confusion.

REAL ESTATE BROKER

A broker is an individual who runs a real estate office. In order to become a broker, one must either 1) work as an agent for a few years, usually for at least two (depending on the state) before he or she can complete additional coursework and sit for a broker's exam. Or 2) be an attorney. In fact, attorneys are the only professionals who are allowed to skip the requirements of being an agent first and move straight in to sitting for a broker's exam. This is because Real Estate Commissions across the country agree that an attorney — by virtue of having passed the state bar and taken courses throughout law school that are related to the practice of real estate — is well equipped to handle the purchase and sale of a property. In fact, as we will see in our discussion of the education requirements of an agent, a real estate agent's training is a mere drop in the bucket when compared to the fact that an attorney must sit through entire semesters' worth of classes such as contracts law, property law, trusts and estates, negotiations, tax law and other courses that are incredibly useful when buying or selling real estate.

In any case, once the agent or attorney has passed the broker's exam, they may decide to take one of three different routes, including:

1. choose to continue working under another broker as an Associate Broker (this is what I have decided to do) or,
2. choose to start their own brokerage or open a franchise office (such as a RE/MAX or Keller Williams) where they decide to work for themselves while not hiring any other agents, or,
3. choose to start a new brokerage or open a franchise and hire agents to work for them. Under this last scenario, the broker may

further choose to only manage the other agents and not handle any more transactions, or they may decide they still want to represent buyers and sellers as agents. Sometimes, brokers decide not to continue representing buyers and sellers since the agents within their office may not like the idea of their broker "competing" with them for business.

Regardless of what option the broker decides to go with, it is important for the seller to know that all listing agreements that you sign to list your house for sale are signed between yourself and the brokerage, not the real estate agent. As such, a lot of liability falls on a broker's shoulders since they own the brokerage. Further, since the brokerage owns all the listings of a specific salesperson, if your salesperson were to change brokerages, your listing would remain with the original brokerage, unless that brokerage was willing to release you from the listing agreement so that you could re-list with the salesperson and their new brokerage.

REAL ESTATE ASSOCIATE BROKER

This is a person who has completed the additional education classes and earned a broker's license but who chooses to work under the management of another broker — again, this was the route I decided to take, for the time being.

REAL ESTATE AGENT

This is a person who has earned a real estate license by completing the state-required coursework and has passed the real estate agent exam. In the state of Maryland, an individual must take a mere 60-hour course that can be completed in person or online, and then they must sit for and pass the exam.

An agent is considered an independent contractor for the broker, as such, there is little oversight as to what work is completed and the quality of the work. In regards to how they get paid, typically, an agent splits a significant portion of his or her commission checks with the broker to continue being affiliated with that brokerage.

REAL ESTATE SALESPERSON

This title is interchangeable with the previous three titles as it is a blanket term used to identify someone who helps clients buy and sell real estate. This term is generally synonymous with the terms real estate broker, associate broker, and real estate agent.

REALTOR®

A REALTOR® is also a real estate agent with the only difference being that they are an active, paying member of the National Association of REALTORS® (NAR), the largest trade association in the United States. Further, the term 'REALTOR®' is a federally registered collective membership mark, which is why the term coexists with the ® symbol.

In order to subscribe to the NAR, a member must subscribe to the REALTOR® Code of Ethics. Thus, the use of the word REALTOR® is meant to demonstrate that the agent agrees to a higher standard. There are 17 Articles in the Code of Ethics, which can be found here.

However, for most consumers, they are in the dark about the fact that the Code of Ethics even exists. In fact, the word "ethics" is ambiguous in nature and can be interpreted in as many different ways as the number of REALTORS® who have sworn to uphold them. And due to this lack of consistency, there is nothing substantial for the consumer to count on or properly enforce.

Nonetheless, the NAR suggests that a REALTOR® must subscribe to their code of ethics. But truth be told, there is no guarantee that a REALTOR® is any more ethical than an unaffiliated real estate agent, since they are both held to the same legal standard. The *legal standard* that all real estate professionals owe their clients, regardless of whether they are an agent or REALTOR®, falls under agency law, which will be discussed in the upcoming chapter known as a fiduciary duty.

Although a person may bring a complaint against a REALTOR® for breach of fiduciary duty, in order for the punishment to be anything more than just a mere slap on the wrist, most states, including Maryland, have found that there must be another claim of action in addition to a breach of duty. For example, the offending REALTORS® behavior must have been incredibly egregious and the client must have incurred some sort of damages due to the REALTORS® actions. Due to this fact, it can be difficult for a victim to find victory in the law, which further exacerbates the fact that there is no easy way to clean up the industry of immoral REALTORS®. This is just one of the ways in which the National Association of REALTORS® (NAR) has failed consumers such as yourself. This is a topic that definitely deserves more attention, which is why we will discuss this in more depth in a later chapter.

DESIGNATIONS: THE ACRONYMS BEHIND A REALTORS® NAME

Before we move on, I would like to take this opportunity to discuss designations. Having a designation means that the REALTOR® took the initiative to take a one to two day course that is offered by the NAR to increase their knowledge in a specific area of real estate. Now, while there is no denying the value in education, for the most part, having a bunch of acronyms behind your name has no real bearing on an agent's abilities. In fact, I have worked with numerous REALTORS® and agents who are very qualified but have not earned a designation. On the other hand, I have also worked with a handful of REALTORS® who have what appears to be the entire alphabet behind their name but, in my humble opinion, should not be practicing real estate.

To prove my point about how inconsequential these designations are, ask any REALTOR® who does not have one of these acronyms behind their name to identify the designations, and I promise you that nine out of ten REALTORS® have no clue what these acronyms stands for. Therefore, you must ask yourself, if people within the industry have no clue what these letters mean, how much value does it *truly* hold for a consumer?

We have covered a lot of ground here as we've just wrapped up the different titles and acronyms provided for real estate professionals and their underlying meaning. Now, it's time to get to the hardcore, nitty-gritty fundamentals of what you should expect from your chosen real estate professional. We are going to start with the fiduciary duties that are owed to you, which can often go completely under the radar of the home seller. But by being privy to these duties, it changes the game and tilts the odds dramatically in your favor, and it sets you up for massive success in selling your home — you will see what I mean by continuing onto the next chapter!

CHAPTER FOURTEEN

❖

FIDUCIARY DUTIES OF A REAL ESTATE PROFESSIONAL TO THE SELLER

At first glance, you may believe that you and your real estate professional have the same goals in mind; you may believe that you both want to sell the property at the highest price possible. But contrary to popular belief, while homeowners will obviously want to sell their home at the highest price possible, an average real estate professional will mainly want to just sell the home in the shortest amount of time. Now, before we move on, I want to emphasize the point that there many agents who truly do want the best outcome for their clients and do want to sell for the highest price. However, it is important to know this information so that you can differentiate between hiring an agent who wants to sell in the shortest amount of time versus the agent who really wants you to receive the highest amount of net proceeds.

The fact that the typical real estate agent may not share the same values as the homeowner in getting the highest price possible may come at a surprise. After all, the higher the price, the higher the agent's commission check will be, right? While this is certainly true, the typical real estate professional realizes that there is a lot more to gain if a property is sold as quickly as possible, since they will be able to focus their attention on to another property.

To illustrate the point of the agent wanting to sell quickly, imagine you place your property on the market and receive an offer than you find less than worthy of accepting. The agent realizes that by rejecting the offer, they may have to spend even more money on advertisements and more time and energy in marketing. Thus, it's a no-brainer that if the agent can sell a property, albeit at a lower price, then they can move on and spend their efforts on the next property, thus making more money.

Since the interests of a homeowner are not always aligned with an agent's, the legal duties that are owed to a homeowner may not be fully met, as the agent is anxious to sell for speed, while the homeowner wants to sell for the maximum amount. Regardless of whether the homeowner and agent have different goals, it is critical for you to understand the duties that are owed to a homeowner, because your agent should always act in *your* best interest.

The concept of having a real estate agent act in your best interests is based on the agency relationship that is created between you and them. As you may remember from the previous chapter in our discussion of real estate brokers, the agency relationship is memorialized when you sign a listing agreement that serves as an agreement of employment between you (the principal) and the brokerage (the agent), not the agent. However, even though the contract is between you and the brokerage, since you will be directly working with the agent, your agent will be the person responsible for acting with the utmost good faith towards you.

Whenever an agency relationship is created, the agent owes the principal a set of fiduciary duties. When the agent is acting as the fiduciary, they are legally required to uphold and act in a manner that is consistent with six specific duties. Among these duties, the agent owes the seller the duty of accounting, care, loyalty, confidentiality, obedience, and disclosure.

Over the years, common and statutory laws regarding the fiduciary responsibilities of agents have evolved. There are new court cases every year in every state that have actually **raised** the standards and expectations of both the clients (the principal) and the courts. Lawsuits against real estate agents are based on a number of different claims, including but not limited to: allegations of negligence, lack of disclosure, and conflict of interest. As such, if these six fiduciary duties are violated or not performed properly by the agent, they may be held liable for damages. In such circumstances, the principal can seek remedies that include refusal to pay compensation, rescission of the listing contract, an action for restitution, and/or an action for losses.

One of the important things to remember about these duties is that many of them are closely related and work synergistically. For instance, loyalty and confidentiality are closely linked. It's easier to establish confidentiality when you have loyalty, as confidentiality is something that naturally flows from being loyal to someone or something. Thus, loyalty and confidentiality are almost like two sides of the same coin. However, while some of the duties are closely linked to one another, they are also just as powerful when viewed in isolation. Now, let's examine each duty in detail.

DUTY OF CARE

Since an agent is a licensed professional, he or she is considered to have the skill, knowledge, and care that are beyond that of an average person. This means that you, as the client, should have an expectation that your agent knows how to advise on price, market your house, handle negotiations, and give relevant advice related to the many other facets of the transaction. You can then logically, and legally, assume that the agent will carry out these duties with care to fulfill your needs. Where an agent's conduct fails to meet this standard of care, the real estate agent may be liable for any damages suffered by you, flowing from the real estate agent's negligence.

How can you know that your agent has acted in a manner that fulfills the standard of care expected of real estate professionals?

In order to determine whether a real estate agent has fulfilled the standard of care, courts will typically look to industry practices, customs, and statutory guidelines in order to measure the agent's conduct against the conduct of a reasonably prudent person in the same profession. It is important to bear in mind that real estate agents are not expected to perform services normally provided by engineers, lawyers, accountants, or other professionals, which fall outside the scope of an agent's license. If concerns arise outside the scope of a broker's knowledge, the agent is expected to give you proper recommendations on how to get the information.

Yet, there are other ways in which your agent can meet the standard of care. First and foremost, they should be readily available and return phone calls and emails promptly. Additionally, your agent should be familiar with the neighborhood and the surrounding geographic area that a home is located. If an agent does not warn the new homeowner of a particular issue relating to the geographic location of a home and it results in a problem for the homeowner in the future, there could be a potential lawsuit.

DUTY OF DISCLOSURE

An agent must disclose to the principal any information that the principle would deem to be material, important, or influential to the process of selling their home. Material facts are those that, if known by the seller, might cause a seller to change his or her actions. Such information may include information affecting the buyer's ability or desire to perform, or any pertinent fact that can influence a seller's decision as to whether to accept or reject a particular offer.

Other pertinent information may include the agent's affiliation with a buyer. For example, if an agent expects to acquire an equitable or beneficial interest in a property, then the agent must specifically disclose the nature of that interest to the seller. Thus, an agent should disclose any familial, personal, or business relationship that he or she has with the buyer.

In fact, as a matter of practice, an agent should avoid the purchase of any property that he or she has listed since they may have become privy to certain pieces of confidential information that the seller may have shared with them through the course of their interactions. There is also a clear conflict of interest between your agent's interests and the principal's interests which can cloud your agent's judgment if you allow your agent to purchase your home, which will be further explored in the next section under the duty of loyalty.

Yet another common piece of information that some agents fail to disclose is the amount of compensation offered to the buyer's agent. For example, if a seller decides to list a property for a total commission of 6%, the agent should be upfront about how that commission is split with the buyers' agent. A seller may be under the impression that the commission will be split equally between the listing agent and the buyer's agent. However, some listing agents may decide to split the commission by giving the buyer's agent 2.5%, which in turn, will allow them to keep 3.5%.

The reason why the apportionment of commission is significant to a seller is because it may negatively impact the actions of buyer's agents. For example, although an ***ethical*** buyer's agents should show ***all*** homes that fit within their clients' needs and desires, some agents may try to talk their clients out of placing offers on particular homes, or even fabricate reasons why a property cannot be shown, all because the buyer's agent's commission for a particular property is lower than all other comparable homes. The average agent only sells four homes per year and, therefore, a buyer's agent will obviously want their client to choose a home that offers the most commission. As a direct result, a seller may experience a significant delay in selling his or her home if the commission offered to the buyer's agent is low when compared to comparable neighboring properties. Therefore, it is wise to find out what percent is typically allocated to the buyer's agents within your neighborhood and to make sure the amount you are offering the buyer's agent is competitive with that amount. This information is readily available to your listing agent and, therefore, it would be prudent to ask so that you may offer the same amount.

Finally, it goes without saying that if an agent is not aware of a particular fact, he or she is not responsible under the duty of disclosure. For example, if a house has a lien on it, the agent will not know about the lien until a title search is conducted and, therefore, there is no duty to disclose until the agent is aware that the lien exists.

DUTY OF LOYALTY

Closely related to the duty to disclose material information regarding the property to the principal is the duty of loyalty. The duty of loyalty prohibits agents from placing their self-interests or the interests of a third party above their principal's interests, without full disclosure to the principal. One prime example of when full disclosure to the principal is required is when the buyer's agent and the seller's agent belong to the same brokerage, more commonly known as dual agency. The concept of dual agency is quite tricky so it deserves a closer examination.

In most states, dual agency is allowed, if both the seller and the buyer give informed consent in writing. Therefore, if Agent A and Agent B both work at XYZ Realty, then the seller must sign a form, acknowledging and consenting to the possibility of dual agency. Under this scenario, it can be argued that since Agent A and Agent B are colleagues, they have a better working relationship with one another and are more likely to be respectful to one another in closing the transaction, which translates to a smoother experience for both the seller and the buyer.

For example, I once represented a buyer, and unfortunately, the seller's agent on the other side was incredibly difficult to work with. He made outrageous demands and was incredibly rude and dismissive, which ultimately led the buyers to believe that these sentiments were coming from the seller.

However, when we were conducting the inspection and had an opportunity to meet the sellers, my client and I realized that the sellers were not the ones who were making the transaction so difficult; instead, it was the listing agent who was unnecessarily complicating matters due to his own ego! I believe that if the listing agent was from the same office as I, we could have had a much more amicable and smooth transaction.

As you can see, dual agency can be beneficial. However, in some states, it is also recognized as dual agency when one agent represents both the seller and the buyer. In my opinion, this type of scenario should be avoided at all costs. When the same agent is representing both you and the buyer, this is often a no-win situation for either party since you both have diametrically adverse goals. The conflict of interest is apparent from the onset; the seller wants to receive the highest price possible for the property, while the buyer would like to purchase the property at the lowest price possible. Even though an agent may feel as though he or she is capable of acting in an unbiased fashion on behalf of both parties, in practice, they would be foolish to do so. This is especially true since an agent in this scenario closely resembles an attorney who attempts to represent both parties in a divorce action — which is impossible and, illegal since the parties in a divorce action have an inherent conflict of interest.

It should also be noted that in many states, including Maryland, this type of scenario is illegal. But what I have seen many listing agents do is that they will submit an offer on behalf of a buyer but will not sign a Buyer Broker Agreement with that buyer which then renders the relationship between the agent and the buyer to that of a "customer" instead of a "client."

The differentiation between a client and a customer is of significance since the duty owed to a client, is higher than that owed to a mere customer. The duties owed to a client include all of these fiduciary duties that we are discussing in this chapter while a duty to the customer means the agent must only act in a manner that is consistent with "honest and fair dealings." However, this differentiation in duty is often never fully explained to either the seller or the buyer. As such, what ends up happening is that the agent often fails to meet their duty of loyalty to the seller since they become more concerned with the fact that if they can close the deal, they would be entitled to receiving both sides of the commission. Additionally, if your agent finds the buyer and submits an offer on their behalf, they may fail to aggressively negotiate on your behalf because again, their self-interest of gaining the full commission may kick in.

For these reasons, make sure that you are fully aware of how dual agency is treated in your state. Additionally, you should specifically ask your agent how they plan to proceed if an unrepresented buyer wants them to submit an offer. On the one hand, you may prefer to have your agent submit the offer on behalf of the buyers since you implicitly trust your agent to represent your interests fully or, you may want that agent to refer that buyer to another agent. Either way, I believe that you and your agent should have a clear understanding of how these situations will be handled so that everyone has clear expectations from the onset. However, let it be known that I would strongly encourage for you to prohibit your agent from submitting an offer on behalf of an unrepresented buyer.

DUTY OF CONFIDENTIALITY

Another component of the loyalty piece is the duty of confidentiality. An agent is obligated to keep confidential and safeguard any information that is provided by you, the principal. By upholding the confidence of the seller, an agent reduces the amount of damaging information that can negatively impact the seller's bargaining position during the course of a negotiation.

An example of when the duty of confidentiality kicks in is when a buyer asks the listing agent as to why the sellers are selling. A seller's motivation for selling can sometimes be deemed confidential, especially if the reason is due to some sort of distress such as an impending foreclosure, divorce, illness, or death. This is because by sharing the reason, it can motivate the buyer to submit a low-ball offer since they are now privy to the information that the sellers are highly motivated and thus, more likely to accept the low-ball offer. Of course, perhaps, you may decide you do not mind if this information is shared with a prospective purchaser — in any case, you should be very clear with your listing agent as to what information is considered confidential versus what information you do not mind being shared.

Yet another piece of information that you may or may not decide that you want shared with a prospective purchaser is whether or not you are willing to sell at a price that is lower than the listed price. Sometimes, a seller will want the agent to inform the prospective buyers that there is room for negotiation. In other situations, while you might share this with your agent, you may not want them to necessarily also share it with the buyers. This is why, again, it is important to be very clear as to what you consider confidential information versus what information you want your agent to discuss with the prospective buyers.

Conversely, the duty of confidentiality does not mean that an agent, who is representing a seller, can withhold known material facts about the condition of the seller's property from prospective buyers. As a friendly reminder, material facts about the condition of a property must *always* be disclosed to a buyer and therefore, fall outside the scope of an agent's duty of confidentiality.

However, duty of confidentiality does extend to protecting digital information in today's cyber world. Real estate agents are given a lot of personal and financial information, and agents have a duty to safeguard that data. Agents must protect their clients' files from hackers and identity thieves by installing security software on their computers and securing paper files in a locked area. If information is hacked because of an agent's negligence, although it may be difficult and expensive to prove, an agent can be held liable.

While we are on the topic of cyber security, it is worth noting the alarming rate at which real estate transactions are being targeted by insidious wire scammers. According to the FBI, cyber criminals involved in the Business Email Compromise (BEC) fraud have collected almost $3.1 billion between January of 2015 and June of 2016 alone! And this type of scam will only continue to rise, unless proper preemptive measures and education systems are enforced.

This type of scam occurs when a hacker breaks into either a consumers email account or into a real estate professional's email account to determine when an upcoming transaction is scheduled to close. The hacker then sends a compromised email to whoever needs to bring money to the closing table. While it is usually the buyer who routinely wires large sums of money to close deals, sellers can also be targeted. This can be the case if a seller owes more than what the property is worth (such as in a short sale), and thus, they have to bring money to the settlement table. Either way, both sellers and buyers are typically not trained to recognize fraudulent emails and can therefore, be easily deceived. In fact, the hacker is taking advantage of the psychology of buyers and sellers since they are both typically very stressed out with moving and everything else that comes with settlement. And as such, they are both unlikely to be scrutinizing every single detail of the transaction, including every email.

In the email, the hacker poses as the real estate professional or the title company with new, fraudulent wiring instructions, urging them to quickly transfer the funds in order to avoid further delays. The new email address may be very similar to the true email address, which is purposely done in order to better deceive the receiver. For example, perhaps the title company uses an email address of name@xyztitlecompany.com. Then, the hacker will create a very similar email address such as name@xyztitlecompany.net. As you can see, the difference between using .com versus .net is incredibly minor but the difference can be absolutely catastrophic. This is because the hacker then sends new wiring instructions that include new routing numbers that belong to the hacker and not to the title company. From there, the funds are either immediately withdrawn or transferred to an overseas account, thus making it close to impossible to trace and recover. For this reason, thousands of sellers and buyers have fallen for this scheme and millions of dollars have been lost.

Due to the complex nature of wire fraud, not only is prosecuting difficult, but recovering the funds are close to impossible. As such, Congress is aggressively trying to pass a bill (H.R. 2205) that would require individuals, corporations, or other non-government entities (such as the real estate industry) that handle sensitive financial account information or nonpublic personal information to encrypt all that information. However, until this regulation is passed, both consumers and professionals should be vigilant and educate themselves in preemptive methods of keeping information safe from hackers.

While the real estate industry is slowly awakening to the significant cyber security risks, in an effort to take a more preventative approach, it is beneficial for you to become more educated about email fraud. To avoid becoming a victim, there are a few ways that you can protect yourself and your information. First and foremost, never send any sensitive financial information via email (including banking information and routing numbers). Also, never wire funds without directly speaking to the listing agent and the title company via a certified telephone number to confirm the wiring instructions. Finally, always go with your instincts and err on the side of being overly cautious. If you receive a suspicious email, do not open it, and if you do, do not click on any links within the email, as this can give the hackers unauthorized access into your entire account. If something does not feel right to you, call the title company or your real estate professional to confirm.

DUTY OF OBEDIENCE

An agent must promptly obey all lawful instructions that the principal gives to the agent. However, no agent is obligated to obey an instruction that violates the law. Therefore, an instruction to not market a property to minority groups, or to misrepresent the condition of a property, both of which are illegal, do not fall under the scope of the duty of obedience.

DUTY OF ACCOUNTING

Agents are obligated to account for all funds that have been entrusted to them by the principal and to not commingle their funds with that of their principals. This duty also extends to any documents, or other personal property that has been entrusted to the agent, such as Power of Attorney documents, deeds, garage door openers, and keys.

Now that we understand that duties that are owed to you by your agent, I would like to spend some time discussing two concepts — one that is relatively new, and another that has been around for decades. The first concept we will discuss is the new discount brokerage model, which is the relatively recent phenomenon. The second concept is what is known as Guaranteed Sales Programs.

CHAPTER FIFTEEN

❖

THINK TWICE BEFORE HIRING A DISCOUNT BROKER

About two years ago, I herniated two of my spinal discs. It happened completely out of the blue — one minute I was walking, and the next, I felt something give out in my back. Within a few hours, I knew my back was seriously injured. A few doctors' visits, X-rays, and an MRI later, it was revealed that two disks in my lower back were herniated — L4 and L5, to be exact. It was a painful period of my life. I couldn't sleep, sit, or conduct most physical activities.

I then began my journey of endless acupuncture visits, three epidural injections, physical therapy, dry needling, and even several homeopathic doctor visits. With every visit, I felt more and more hopeless, thinking, *"Is this what my life is going to be like from now on?"* Nothing seemed to work, and I was absolutely miserable. Surgery seemed to be the only option left. I knew surgery had the potential to be life changing — it could go either terribly wrong, where I would continue to experience pain, or it could put me back on the road to recovery, and towards living a normal life again. Ultimately, the surgeon entrusted to perform the procedure could make or break me — no pun intended. And so I embarked on the journey of interviewing surgeons. I interviewed a total of six surgeons, until I finally found one with the credentials, experience, and empathy that I felt would best help ease my pain.

Some people might be thinking, *"You interviewed SIX doctors?! Who has time for that?!"* I know that six doctors might seem like one too many but I knew that the chosen doctor would be instrumental in placing me on a path towards recovery, and therefore, it was not a decision I was going to take lightly.

So what does this all have to do with your home? I want you to realize that selling your home with the wrong agent, like picking the wrong doctor, can be incredibly painful. For example, if a surgery like the one that was performed on me was not done properly, the medical condition could have gotten worse, cost me more money in the future, or could have made the recovery process longer. Similarly, an agent can also worsen an already emotional process, net you less money in your pocket, and to top it all off, they might take a longer time to sell your property. This is why you should interview and vet several real estate agents.

When it comes to the value that the right agent provides, discount brokerages portray an inaccurate perception of value to the sellers. To be clear, I am referring to brokerages and agents offering to sell your home for a *significantly* discounted fee. I can understand that an agent may want to stay competitive, but with an agent who quotes you a price that is far off from any other agent, the first question to ask is, *"How can they afford such a price reduction in their fees and still remain profitable?"*

While most sellers don't need advice about the potential perils they will face by putting their home on the market with this type of operation, it most definitely necessitates a closer examination. When an agent meets with a seller, it is the agent's duty to be able to clearly explain and differentiate their skills from the waves of other agents to avoid becoming commoditized. But when an agent is unable to demonstrate their value, they have to resort to dropping their price in order to gain business. When this happens, sellers may *feel* like they are getting a deal, and let's face it, everyone wants a good deal.

But at what cost?

When agents or brokers begin to play the price game, they are slashing prices in an effort to gain listings. Most agents and brokerages that adopt the lets-drop-the-price-to-make-the-deal-happen model do so at the cost of quality. Pure and simple, the real estate industry cannot afford to cut corners in quality, because it is already an industry that is ridden with negative stigma. When price becomes the main source of differentiation between real estate companies, it becomes impossible for the consumer to view the agent as anything more than a commodity, which a good agent is not. And when an agent is viewed as a commodity, it becomes impossible to build a trusting relationship, which is dangerous in an industry that is already soaked with mistrust.

To see how price impacts quality, let us focus our attention to the company of Wal-Mart. There is no debating that the founder of Wal-Mart, Sam Walton, built a widely successful company — with yearly revenues of around $500 **billion** while employing nearly 2 **million** people. There is also no debating that Wal-Mart was able to reach this level of success by offering lower prices than that of their competitors.

But again, at what cost?

Wal-Mart's prioritization of low prices above quality has exposed the company to legal problems — nearly 5,000 lawsuits a year. Almost every lawsuit was born from Wal-Mart's obsession with offering low prices. These legal battles frequently stem from unfair labor practices, including multiple charges of locking employees in stores overnight to clean the store, and forcing employees to work long hours without breaks. Therefore, the example of Wal-Mart as a discount retailer illustrates the lackluster behind price slashing since the savings enjoyed by consumers were at the cost of the mistreatment experienced by the employees of Wal-Mart. Similarly, while Wal-Mart cut corners by mistreating their employees, discount brokers are able to cut corners with comparable yet less apparent tactics.

Now before we discuss further, I do want to admit that technology has significantly changed the face of real estate and has made it much easier to conduct business. And as such, I do believe that these changes should be reflected in the commissions charged. But for now, I want to limit my discussion of discount brokers in order to highlight where most of these discount brokers are cutting costs and how they are able to maintain a profitable business so that you may decide for yourself as to whether or not they are the best option for you.

The first matter of discussion is the skill of the agent. Think of it like this, would an experienced and renowned orthopedic surgeon discount his or her services? Generally speaking, health services in the United States are only discounted when the doctor is inexperienced (and needs patients to practice on), undesired, or not 'good enough' to compete with doctors who charge higher rates. Knowing that the health industry in the United States is expensive, a doctor with low rates might not be the one you want operating on you. And in fact, when I was deciding on the orthopedic surgeon for my back surgery, I certainly took their pricing into consideration and chose not to hire the doctor with the lowest fee. Likewise, the same logic applies when hiring an agent who will handle the single largest investment of your entire life. If a real estate agent quotes you fees that are *astonishingly low*, it is a reasonable deduction that the quality of the agent may also be low.

One main area of skill that is clearly lacking for a discount agent is negotiation. If an agent is willing to reduce their own commissions from the outset, without any negotiation, you have to question their skills in the negotiation department. At the end of the day, you are hiring someone for the sole task of netting you the most amount of money for the largest investment of your life, and if they lack the fortitude to negotiate on their own behalf to justify their own fees, how are they going to negotiate on your behalf? When a buyer pressures the listing agent to reduce prices, discount agents will not negotiate with same rigor as a full commission agent.

Yet another way that discount brokers and agents fail their clients is through misleading advertisements. Discount brokers and agents often advertise a significantly lower commission, but the advertised commission percentage only reflects the fee for the listing agent, and it usually does not include the commission charged for the buyer's agent. This information is often conveniently not mentioned up front, simply for the purpose of capturing clients. Therefore, when a relationship begins under these false pretenses, it is difficult to foster a relationship rooted in trust later on.

Furthermore, many home sellers fail to realize that they will actually lose money by hiring a discount agent. This is because agents affiliated with discount companies often have lower average sales prices than agents working at full service and full commission brokerages for similar properties. To understand why average sales prices are often lower when listed with a discount broker, it helps to examine how the commission structure for a real estate agent works.

While many sellers understand that agents charge a commission, they are sometimes unclear about how that commission is divided after it has been earned. Let's begin by assuming a discount agent's fee is 1%. Automatically, the agent needs to set aside 30% towards taxes since taxes are not deducted from commission checks. Then, the agent may need to pay a desk fee in order to pay for technology tools, printing, and an administrative assistant. Then, the broker may take a portion of the commission, which can be anywhere between 20-50%. Then, the agent has to consider the cost of gas, error and omissions insurance, association dues, lock box fees, and Multiple Listing Service fees.

You may say, this is all just the cost of doing business, but let's look at some real numbers.

According to the Census Bureau, the average sales price of a home in the United States is approximated at $300,000. Let's assume the listing fee for a discount broker is 1%, which would be $3,000. Conservatively, taxes account for 30%, bringing the earned commission down to $2,100. Then, that amount is split with the broker, which can be up to 50%, thus bringing the commission down to $1,050. Finally, after all the technological tools and other expenses are paid, the agent would be lucky to take home $500 from that 1% listing fee. Sadly, this leaves very little for the agent to live on! In turn, the agent will need to do much more volume and will need to sell many homes in order to make a living. However, volume is not necessarily an option, since according to the National Association of Realtors (NAR), the average agent only sells four homes per year! With this type of business model, agents would likely have to take on another job, which would render them a part-time real estate agent; meaning their focus is not on properly following market trends or staying up to date on the laws and regulations pertaining to real estate.

Even after the noted deductions, we have not yet even accounted for any costs associated to marketing your home — which is exactly where a discount agent will withhold spending money on. As a result, a less robust marketing plan translates into fewer eyeballs on your home. When fewer potential buyers are aware that your property exists, there will be less demand for your home, which will then result in a lower sales price. When you do the math, it is clear that by hiring a full-service agent or broker, you will likely net more than you would with a discount broker. These discount agents and brokers reduce prices because they believe it will boost their perceived value; however, this pricing strategy does not reach the overall goals of the sellers, who want to net the highest amount possible.

Although discounts are a legitimate tactic in driving business, the challenge is in maintaining quality. Do not get distracted by the pricing game, it will not serve your end goals of netting the highest sales price well. Instead, invest your efforts on finding and building a relationship with an agent who has the negotiation skills and marketing tools that will yield you the highest sales price possible. Bottom line, in the case of a discount broker, you really get what you pay for. However, I do not believe that now is the time to be penny wise and pound-foolish.

Now that we have a clear understanding of discount brokers, let's focus our attention to yet another area within the real estate industry that I believe is often unclear to home sellers – Guaranteed Sales Programs.

CHAPTER SIXTEEN

❖

THE TRUTH ABOUT GUARANTEED SALES PROGRAMS

Over the past year, any time I am doing anything less than mentally stimulating - driving, working out, or even relaxing in the sauna - I pop in my headphones and listen to podcasts. For those of you unfamiliar with podcasts, they are audio files that can be downloaded onto your phone, computer, or other electronic device. You can listen to them at any time, and they include topics ranging from investing, dating, entrepreneurial advice, and just about any other topic that tickles your fancy. Since realizing my general affinity for the podcast scene, I've since narrowed down my listening and plugged into real estate related podcasts, which keeps me both inspired and informed.

Late one night, earlier in my real estate career, I was up listening to a podcast. The host was interviewing a fast-talking, top-producing real estate agent. As I listened, my fascination grew. Maybe it was because he had a knack for telling stories; he started his career in real estate fresh out of high school, and through determination and grit, he was able to create a team of over 25 agents that worked for him. Impressive. Or maybe, it was because of his charismatic nature. Whatever the reason, I was hooked. But he soon turned to the topic of his "Guaranteed Sales Program." And as he began discussing the details, it dawned on me that his "Guaranteed Sales Program" wasn't a guarantee at all — it was a classic bait and switch.

If you are unfamiliar with these types of "guarantees," let me tell you that they come in all shapes and sizes. Typically, it includes an agent loudly and proudly proclaiming, "If we don't sell your home, we will buy it!" or "We will guarantee your home is sold in 30 days," or, some other variation of an enticing offer. Regardless of how it's phrased, the premise hinges on the fact that the agent promises that the property will be sold, even if it means that the agent has to buy it. While such a claim may seem harmless, I strongly believe that there are several problems with this "promise."

But before we get into all the different problems, I want to extend my apology to all the sellers who have personally experienced this type of fraudulent, misleading, and gimmicky marketing scam. This may sound overly dramatic, but the reality is that there are agents who unfortunately do not understand what it means to be ethical and honest.

> **Instead, they have become adept at convincing unsuspecting consumers that *their scams are solutions.***

But as you will see, these bait and switch tactics cause financial damage to good people, causing them to leave thousands of dollars at the door.

First and foremost, all of these types of programs come with fine print, which will include a multitude of conditions and caveats. And of course, since the agent writes the fine print, these conditions will always serve the agent's interests so that ultimately, the agent will not be legally bound to buying your house. In fact, I'll let you in on a little secret: all the training programs that teach these types of Guaranteed Sales Programs, also teach the agent what they need to include in the fine print so that they never have to follow through and actually purchase the house, if it doesn't sell. Because, let's face it, unless the agent comes from an incredibly wealthy family or otherwise has a large pot of gold sitting somewhere, buying homes left and right is just not feasible.

Here are some possible loopholes that may be incorporated into Guaranteed Sales Programs:

- Most commonly, you will find that the terms of the guarantee will dictate that if the house doesn't sell within a certain time frame, the seller must agree to a pre-determined price reduction. Often times, these price reductions require the seller to go so low that they are practically giving their home away!

- Or, there will be a term stating that the seller has to agree to purchase a significantly more expensive home through the same agent.
- Or, there will be a term that requires the seller to purchase a property that is listed by the agent, thus, drastically restricting the seller's options of homes to buy. Also, bear in mind that as previously discussed in Chapter Fourteen, when a seller is forced to purchase another one of the agents' listings, the agents fiduciary duties towards the seller weakens. This is because now, the roles have switched as the seller is the buyer and the agent only owes you a duty of fair and honest dealings to a buyer since they are considered a customer and not a client. And therefore, the agent will no longer owe you the fiduciary duties that we previously discussed.
- Or, there could be a certain price point in which the guarantee is no longer valid. For example, they are only willing to buy the home if it is below $200k and therefore, if the value of your home is above that amount, you will not qualify.
- Or, the seller must agree to stage their property, which can cost thousands of dollars.
- Or, the seller must conduct an inspection and repair any and all issues that are discovered

As you can see, every single one of these conditions are beneficial for the agent, NOT the seller.

As discussed earlier, agents owe sellers fiduciary duties, which require the agent to look out for the best interest of the seller. Needless to say, the best interest of the seller is the sale of his or her home at the highest price possible. Sellers rely on their agents for sound advice regarding the value of their homes. However, when an agent offers these so-called "guarantees," the seller will likely not be able to obtain a fair price, much less, the highest price possible for their home. Instead, the agent will probably have to list the property under (often WAY under) the current market value of the property to avoid meeting the terms of the "guarantee." With that being said, what are the odds that the seller would receive accurate information regarding the price of their home? Low — very low. In fact, I guarantee the list price they suggest will be much less than what you could reasonably expect a buyer to pay.

With all of this in mind, how often do you think agents uphold their end of the deal and actually purchase the property? I am inclined to say: very, very rarely. When agents actually do buy the property, do you think the agent is just going to move into the property and call it home? The answer is a very resounding: NO! Instead, the agent will turn around and place the property on the market and sell it for tens of thousands of dollars more. This is because the agent will price it at the fair market value, which is the price it would have been sold had you not agreed to the Guarantee Sales Program. So ask yourself, how would it make you feel knowing that the agent will sell your property for a profit, when that same profit could have gone in your pocket?

At this point, you may be thinking, who in their right mind would agree to such a thing?

Truth is, agents are not offering these programs with the expectation that many people will sign up. Rather, the ultimate and true goal of the program is to only spark enough interest among the seller in order for him or her to want to contact the agent to learn more about the program. This inquiry then becomes an opportunity for the agent to generate more business. This is exactly why these programs have become popular among some agents.

These types of programs have become so effective in generating leads that many top producing agents actually purchase endorsements from celebrities, like Barbara Corcoran and Glenn Beck. And this is because many people, including home sellers, trust celebrity endorsements as they think, "these celebrities are rich and they can use any product or service they want, so whatever they are endorsing must be good, especially since they are putting their reputation on the line to promote it, right?" While that might be true in some cases, in the case of Guaranteed Sales Programs, I think a more compelling reason is that the celebrity merely views the endorsement for what it is, an opportunity to be paid.

Furthermore, since Guaranteed Sales Programs have gained popularity among top-producing agents, there are many lower producing agents who now try to emulate and use these types of techniques as part of their own marketing strategy. As such, this herd mentality has only further perpetuated the use of this scheme. To put this all in perspective, Willie Sutton, a famous bank robber, once said, when asked why he robbed banks, "[Well,] that's where the money is." And that's exactly what these agents think when they see the top-producing agents using this tactic: that these Guaranteed Sales Programs are where the money is. Sadly but clearly, these agents are more interested in winning business in a shady manner than taking care of their clients.

Yet another reason that Guaranteed Sales Programs have continued to exist is because the truth is, there will always be sellers who need to sell quickly, guaranteed. In other words, this is a desperate seller and desperate times can call for desperate measures. However, quite frankly, I believe that a desperate home seller is still better off selling their home without the use of a Guaranteed Sales Program. This is because if you are going to list the home for a price that is below market value, you can always rest assured that buyers will jump at the opportunity to buy that home. Simply put, no matter what kind of market we are in, homes that are priced way below the current market value will always sell quickly.

Now, to be clear, despite the aforementioned criticism, I have nothing personally against an agent who uses a Guaranteed Sale Program. The type of agent who has to resort to these types of morally gray area tactics are at best, average agents. I am not interested in average agents, and you shouldn't be either. In fact, when an agent uses one of these programs, you may want to thank them since they have made it easier for you, a savvy seller, to avoid hiring that particular agent, as you can see through the gamesmanship.

But what does bother me about these types of programs is that they reinforce negative stereotypes of agents and the real estate industry as a whole. At the end of the day, these types of programs predominantly serve the agent in growing their business and not the seller in selling their home for the highest amount possible. With this being said, it is my hope that with this newfound knowledge, you will be better situated to exercise discernment in the choice of your agent.

Now, if you have decided that you still want to work with a real estate professional, in the upcoming chapter, we will examine how you can interview and hire a stellar agent versus just the average, run of the mill agent. Additionally, we will examine how hiring a real estate attorney can further protect your interests.

CHAPTER SEVENTEEN

❖

CHOOSING THE RIGHT PROFESSIONAL: THE REAL ESTATE AGENT

Warren Buffet has been attributed with coining the idea that being born into a supportive and loving family means that you have won the "fallopian tube lottery." As an adult, I wholeheartedly agree and realize how fortunate I am to have won the lottery based on that definition. However, as a young teenaged girl, I would have argued that the definition of having won the "fallopian tube lottery" was having a mother who was (and is!) an amazingly talented hair stylist. Because for any awkward teenage girl, your hair is closely tied to your self-confidence and by having 24/7 access to a person who could color, tease, layer, and style my hair at a moment's notice, was one of the greatest parts of my adolescence.

Now, although my mom was and continues to be the most talented stylist I have ever known, I was shocked to learn about the requirements she needed to meet in order to become a beautician. Can you believe that in order for her to become a cosmetologist, she needed to complete 1500 hours of hands-on training before she was able to sit for the exam that ultimately granted her the license to practice in a salon?!

If those numbers do not jolt you a bit, let me draw a comparison for you. As mentioned earlier, in Maryland, the real estate licensure class is a whopping 60 hours in order to be granted the responsibility of handling an asset that constitutes the largest portion of a person's estate, earned with sweat equity: your home. Put differently, a bad haircut will eventually grow out but you may never recuperate from the loss of thousands of dollars by picking the wrong agent.

Worried yet? It gets better.

You may think that because they are licensed agents that they have a clear understanding of ethics, fiduciary duties, confidentiality, and have a strong moral code. You may think that they have become overnight mini-attorneys with a thorough understanding of property law, contracts, and a strong sense of negotiation. You may think that if they are not getting the training needed within those 60 hours, that surely, their brokerages are conducting some sort of apprenticeship program to continue preparing them. (HINT: many brokerages do not offer any type of additional training!)

You may think these things but I know you don't.

This is because a recent public opinion poll showed that REALTORS® are among the least trusted professions. This probably has to do with the fact that any sales environment where the salespersons salary is solely dependent upon a commission based upon a percentage of the HIGHEST price paid by the buyer does NOT bring out the best in people. Never has, never will.

With all of this being said, I believe it is safe to assume that you and I are both well aware of the reputation of agents — they are viewed as basic facilitators to the transaction who often place their self-interests above their clients' best interests and who are largely overpaid. Often, the inherent distrust by the consumer of real estate professionals is rooted on past experiences where agents have let down their clients.

This leads me to the question of, what leads smart and talented real estate agents to commit unethical acts where they place their own interests before their clients?

This question is fascinating and I believe it is deeply rooted in psychology. Now, I am no psychologist, nor do I play one on TV, but perhaps it has to do with the Pygmalion Effect, which is often referred to as the power of expectation. The Pygmalion Effect is the idea that the way that people are seen and treated influences the way they act. And as we can see based on the polls, a real estate agent is automatically distrusted before they even speak a word, and hated before they have even met with their potential client. Therefore, the fact that agents are perceived as one of the least trusted professions could be a leading reason as to why agents partake in questionable practices.

Alternatively, a more compelling reason as to why the agent may choose to act unethically has to do with the theory that "desperate times call for desperate measures." Simply put, since the barrier to entry into the profession is so low, with only needing a high school degree (or its equivalent with a GED), 60 hours of classes, and the passage of a 90-minute exam, the number of active agents has reached ridiculously high levels. As a result, it is understandable that there are far fewer sales per agent, meaning, much less income. In fact, according to the 2016 National Association of REALTORS® Member Profile, there are nearly 1.2 million REALTORS® nationwide, and due to the increasing number of agents, the median gross income of REALTORS® fell from $45,800 in 2014 to $39,200 in 2015.

Clearly, as more competition has entered the real estate industry, real estate agents are increasingly faced with the decision of leaving the industry all together as they are not making ends meet. As a result, agents are undoubtedly becoming increasingly more desperate than ever to make sure that a transaction will reach the settlement table where they get paid. And in my opinion, nothing can hurt you more in the sale (and even purchase) of your next real estate transaction than the desperation of your chosen agent.

Given the grim statistics discussed above, the average real estate agent could be just one real estate transaction away from unemployment. When one reaches that level of hopelessness and despair, even a person with the strictest moral compass can quickly begin to rationalize a "little" white lie or an omission from telling the whole truth. So even though an agent may owe you the highest standard of care as your fiduciary agent (which we discussed in Chapter Fourteen), the decision between right and wrong can quickly become muddled.

But regardless of why normally moral people make unsound decisions, the important thing to bear in mind is that it does happen and it can happen to you. And until there is any significant reform, real estate transactions will remain mired in a certain level of graft, dishonesty, and corruption that taints the entire industry. This is why it is more important than ever for you to do your own due diligence when choosing your agent.

Unless you take the time to shield yourself with the proper knowledge of what to look out for when picking a real estate agent, you could face unwanted frustrations in your next real estate transaction. There are masses of marginal agents that are threatening the credibility of the entire real estate industry. And since desperate times call for desperate measures, it is your job to begin holding real estate agents accountable.

So now that we understand the importance of choosing a good agent, let's dive in and discuss how you can go about picking the right real estate agent! By asking a few good questions on the front end, you can save yourself a lot of time and frustration on the back end while also monumentally increasing your chances of success.

I believe that, although referrals are best when it comes to deciding who you want to work with, if you have no other choice and are left with having to find someone on your own, I have included a few interview tactics that I believe will help you in finding the most experienced and trained agent.

HOW TO CHOOSE A CONSUMER-CENTRIC EXPERT ADVISOR

Before we get into the two specific traits that are unique to expert advisors, it is important to know about the first red flag when conducting your interviews. Every single transaction is unique in its own way and, with that, there are certain nuisances that the agent should be aware of. Therefore, even though you should be asking questions of the agent, if there is a lack of a two-way conversation and the agent is not asking questions about your particular situation, this is an absolute red flag that should not be ignored.

Specifically, an agent should take a consumer-centric approach in that they should be asking you about your motivation to sell, what your desired time line is for selling, what your mortgage balance is, and how much you need to net to avoid having to short sale the property. By learning about your specific needs, wants, and expectations, your agent can become more consumer-centric by devising a plan that fits your unique circumstances. However, unfortunately for consumers, the real estate industry is a strongly narcissistic industry and thus, most professionals are agent-centric and not consumer-centric. Just take a look at any real estate professional's personal marketing efforts — more likely than not, they have marketed themselves #1 in *something* and they usually have their face plastered all over their marketing materials. This is all for the sole purpose of gaining more future business. As such, an agent who spends a great deal discussing themselves and who doesn't take the time to learn more about your circumstances will be more likely to have a "one size fits all" marketing approach that is ineffective in today's dynamic market.

Further, an agent-centric real estate professional will only want to share about themselves and will most likely prioritize their self-interests over your interests. To clarify, I mean that you should be wary of an agent whose main intention is to list your property for the sole purpose of being able to further market themselves. This is because the truth of the matter is that a buyer is never going to purchase the property because of who the agent is, they are going to purchase it because the agent had the right tools and processes in place to give your property maximum exposure.

In addition to not hiring an agent-centric individual, I believe that there are other traits that separate a traditional agent from an expert advisor. Since the real estate industry includes aspects of being both a results-driven industry and a service-based industry, an expert advisor should be able to meet the demands of both. First and foremost, in order to fulfill the results-driven demands, your agent should have a comprehensive marketing plan, which occurs before the house even hits the market. Secondly, in order to satisfy the service-based demands, your chosen agent should have a team of experts in which he or she works with as a team to make sure the transaction is successful and smooth.

I am not going to spend any time discussing how your agent should be marketing your property, as I discuss that at length in the For Sale By Owner Edition of this book, which you can find on the companion website for this book along with all the other resources at http://www.sellyourhomewithconfidencebook.com. But as a general guideline, you will want to ask the agent for the addresses of the last five to ten properties they have sold. By entering those addresses into any search engine, you should be able to readily find the quality of the pictures and videos and any other marketing tools they may have used. If their marketing strategy for their previous properties does not appeal to you, then that is an easy way to avoid using that agent.

Now, I would like to take some time to discuss the importance of the agent having a team of experts in place. Running a successful real estate business requires an agent to wear multiple hats. For example, the agent is expected to be a master marketer, a tough negotiator, a creative graphic designer, and an accountant. Therefore, you will want to choose an agent who is committed to investing in additional training above and beyond the basic real estate license. However, the real difference between success and failure is having a solid team, so that rather than having one agent who performs all of the tasks associated with a real estate transaction, you have a group of specialists working for you.

> **Helen Keller once said, "Alone we can do so little, together we can do so much."**

In real estate, the same holds true. By hiring an agent who leads a team of experts (such as a transaction manager, a professional photographer and videographer, and an assistant) can really help expedite the behind the scenes process, which significantly enhances the client experience. To put it in perspective, when a real estate agent works alone, they have to juggle several different responsibilities including showing properties to buyers, prospect for new business, market listings, organize and attend listing appointments, manage the properties that are under contract, provide sellers with feedback, and return emails and phone calls. So you can hire one agent who tries to do all these things himself with a higher likelihood of something going amiss, or you can choose to sell your home with an agent who has effectively recruited and properly trained a team of experts.

Having a team means that your calls will, more likely than not, never go unanswered because there are multiple people looking out for you. And trust me, you're going to want calls returned in a timely fashion because, when there is a problem or an opportunity that suddenly presents itself, you will want an agent who can react as quickly as possible.

Alternatively, if your agent is not able to keep up with the issues or opportunities because they are too busy dealing with trivial tasks, you can begin to feel anxious and rightfully so! This is why it is important to ask the agent what protocols they have in making sure that they can quickly address any issues and or opportunities. Finally, keep in mind that the cost to you is the same whether you have a team or a solo agent helping you. As such, hiring an agent who works with the support of a team behind them becomes a no-brainer since you significantly increase the odds of having a positive experience.

Yet another crucial detail you must pay attention to is pricing. If you are interviewing several agents and a majority give you a list price that are all the same but then another agent comes in and says they can get you a price that is exponentially higher than all the other agents' prices, RUN from that agent. This is the number one tactic I have seen agents use in order to secure the listing, only to have the property sit on the market until there are several price reductions and you reach a point where you are now selling the home for much less than if you had just priced it according to the market.

I hope these suggestions help you in deciding whom you choose to represent you but now, let's discuss two other professionals who are just as important as the agent you use to represent you.

CHAPTER EIGHTEEN

❖

CHOOSING THE RIGHT PROFESSIONAL: THE REAL ESTATE ATTORNEY

So now that you have chosen the real estate agent that will be listing your home, you're all set, right?

Well, as you saw in Chapter 8 where we discussed vicarious liability, by working with an untrained agent, they may expose you to more liability and harm than good. So the answer to the above question should be, "No!"

Often times, home sellers become so overwhelmed with the idea of selling and everything that they must get in order before placing the home on the market that they fail to realize that the *first* professional they should always speak to is an attorney. In fact, in some states, an attorney is required to be physically present or to have some type of involvement in the real estate settlement. While the list of states that require the involvement of an attorney are subject to change with the passing of new legislation, the states that require the involvement of an attorney on some level currently include: Alabama, Connecticut, Delaware, District of Columbia, Florida, Georgia, Kansas, Kentucky, Maine, Maryland, Massachusetts, Mississippi, New Hampshire, New Jersey, New York, North Dakota, Pennsylvania, Rhode Island, South Carolina, Vermont, Virginia and West Virginia.

Now, you may be wondering, "*Do I need a real estate attorney to sell my house?*" The short answer is, "*It depends.*" After all, you are selling perhaps the single largest investment that you will likely ever own and, as we discussed in Part One of this book, one misstep could land you in a legal nightmare. As such, it would be wise to have the involvement of an attorney from the onset in order to greatly reduce your chances of finding yourself named as a defendant.

But the number one reason why you should hire an attorney is because the attorney is the ONLY person in the entire transaction that is truly on your side. The unfortunate truth is that everyone else, including your agent, is looking out for themselves and their paychecks.

> **Additionally, an attorney is not only an essential advocate for you, but they are typically the most educated and knowledgeable of all the professionals you will be working with.**

It is also worth mentioning that neither a real estate agent, a lender, nor a title agent are attorneys and, as such, they are not trained or able to give any legal or financial advice. To do so would constitute as practicing law without a license, which is **against the law**. In fact, an agent could find him or herself liable if they provide you with any legal advice, assuming that they are not also a licensed attorney. For example, if you decide to waive a clause on the Purchase Agreement, your agent can only advise you against it, but they cannot speak to the legal ramifications of such a decision. Therefore, you should expect your agent to recommend that you to seek the advice of a real estate attorney to help with the transaction.

Your attorney will act as the watchdog for both the transaction and for you since they have the unique ability to analyze the legality of the transaction and to spot red flags with your other chosen professionals. And by speaking to an attorney before you place your home on the market, you will have the ability to draw upon their expertise if you ever find yourself in a situation where you are not sure how to move forward. For these reasons, it is important to at least have an initial consultation with an attorney before placing the home on the market.

THE ROLE OF AN ATTORNEY

By speaking to an attorney *before* you hire an agent, you will experience a smooth and successful sale as the attorney may identify legal landmines *before* they become major disasters later down the line. Here are a few examples in which you may need an attorney for the real estate transaction:

- Ability to amend the names on title as well as how title is held if personal situations have occurred such as a divorce or marriage.
- Ability to advise on whether or not you should reserve the right of first refusal on a future sale.
- Ability to advise on whether you can or should offer owner financing to a prospective buyer.
- Ability to resolve any title issues such as liens or encumbrances.
- Ability to draft a Lease Back Agreement if you need to stay in the property once you have sold it to a purchaser.
- Ability to help in the eviction process of a problematic tenant in order to then place your property on the market for sale.

It is advisable to collaborate with an attorney before the sale of your home so that you can avoid common problems and have peace of mind. Yet the single most important reason why you will want to have an attorney on speed dial is to have them review the offer that a potential purchaser is presenting. Once the offer becomes approved and signed by you, the offer becomes known as the Purchase Agreement. The Purchase Agreement is the single most important document in the transaction as it dictates all the conditions and requirements that must be met before settlement. These conditions typically include the requirement of a number of inspections, an appraisal, a policy of title insurance, and approval of financing. There may also be conditions stating that the purchase is contingent on the sale of another property. Thus, it is advisable to have an attorney explain the specific provisions of the contract so that you are not only making knowledgeable and informed decisions, but so that you also have the opportunity to make any changes or additions to reflect your specific desires. Additionally, an attorney can determine whether all contingencies of the Purchase Agreement have been satisfied in accordance with their instructions.

As a general tip, in the event that the buyer is placing an expiration date to their offer and you must sign before having the opportunity to review the offer with your lawyer, it would be prudent to include a contingency stating, "This contract is contingent on review and approval by the seller's attorney to occur within seven business days of the last dated signature on this contract" — or some variation of this.

Moreover, since the closing process and the documents can be confusing and complex, an attorney may be consulted with right before settlement. A seller's attorney can be helpful by reviewing the deed, mortgage instruments, and the proposed settlement statement that the title company has prepared prior to closing. The settlement statement indicates the debits and credits to the buyer and seller, and an attorney can be helpful in explaining the nature, amount, and fairness of these computations and general closing costs. Specifically, an attorney can make certain that the computations of the closing costs are correct and that they are reflective of what was negotiated within the Purchase Agreement. An attorney can also help you navigate any last minute disputes about delivering possession or any last minute adjustments to the settlement statement.

Finally, in order to have a smoother settlement, an attorney can attend and supervise the closing in order to protect your interests. And as mentioned earlier in this chapter, it is important for you to note that the settlement attorney that is hired by the title company does not have a fiduciary duty to you and, as such, they do not have a duty to protect your interests. This is a point of confusion for many sellers, as they mistakenly believe that the attorney for the title company somehow represents them and their interests. Truth is, while the title company has an interest in fostering a successful sale, they cannot and do not advise sellers on their legal rights. We will discuss the role of the title company in more depth in the following chapter.

Clearly, there are many ways in which hiring an attorney can be beneficial. However, the method in which you proceed to find and interview the right attorney can be a daunting task, especially if you do not personally know a real estate attorney, nor the right questions to ask up front.

FINDING AND INTERVIEWING YOUR REAL ESTATE ATTORNEY

Before we discuss some general tips on where to find a good attorney and which questions you should ask, we need to think about jurisdiction. Generally speaking, lawyers are limited to practicing law within the state(s) that they are licensed in. As such, if you live in one state but the property you are selling, perhaps an investment property or vacation home is in another state, you will want to consult with an attorney who is licensed in the same state as where the property is located. Real estate law is hyper localized which is why cross-jurisdictional practice of real estate law is frowned upon. So even though you may want to hire cousin Joe who lives next door to you in Ohio, but the property is in Maryland, be ready for cousin Joe to be unwilling and unable to advise you.

How do you find a good real estate attorney? In searching for a good lawyer, I believe that again, much like finding a good real estate agent, referrals are always best. Start by asking friends, family, and business associates to see if they have worked with a real estate attorney in the past and if they recommend that person (or not so that you know to steer clear of that attorney!). And if you are working with a REALTOR®, they should also have a list of names that they may refer you to. You may also want to reach out to your county bar association who can provide you with a referral list. You can start by visiting the American Bar Association website.

Another good place to find a good attorney is online. A quick Google search will yield you many results where you can explore their websites and reviews so that you can get a feel for their personality and style. Like most professionals, there are some attorneys who you will immediately vibe with, while there will also be others who you can immediately rule out based on the information you find online. Either way, due to the complexities involved in real estate law, make sure that real estate is one of, if not their only, practice areas. Now, assuming you were able to narrow down your top three to five attorneys, you will want to speak with them and ask them very pointed questions.

When calling their office, you may want to start the conversation like this:

> *Hi, my name is_____. I was referred to your office by _____(or if you found them through an online search, mention which site). I am interested in selling my home, located at_____. I have a handful of questions I would like to ask the attorney to make sure they handle my type of transaction; does the attorney have a few minutes?*

At this point, unless the attorney themselves answered the call, the secretary will do one of three things, they will either transfer you to the attorney or, they will take down your information and have the attorney contact you at a later time (this is the most common of the three options) or, they will let you proceed with your questions. In my opinion, there are four major questions you will want answered to make certain that the attorney is a good fit for you and your transaction.

> 1. *I am interested in having an attorney to consult with during the sale of my home, how many real estate transactions have you handled?*

In answering this question, you will want to make sure that the attorney specializes in real estate matters and not in all legal matters. Real estate is a very specific practice area of the law as each jurisdiction has it's own statutes, codes, and regulations. As such, you will want to make sure that the attorney handling your transaction has knowledge about those specific laws. By being familiar with real estate transactions in the jurisdiction where the property is located, the attorney will be able to foresee issues before they happen and if an issue has already occurred, they will be able to resolve them.

With this being said, I would caution against working with a general practice attorney who may do a little family law, a little criminal law, a little personal injury, and a little bit of real estate. Real estate law is too complex and the regulations change far too often for a jack-of-all-trades attorney to stay current on.

2.   *How much should I expect to pay for your services?*

You should always ask the lawyer to explain to you what fees you can reasonably expect to pay. To handle a simple real estate transaction that does not have other legal issues attached to it can be relatively straightforward. As such, your attorney should be able to provide you with a written quotation of the legal services they will provide, along with an estimate of the total costs you can expect to pay. By doing so, you will be able to eliminate some attorneys based on price. While it will be easy to eliminate an attorney who charges too much, you will also want to be aware of an attorney who quotes you a very low fee. This is because the low quote could be a way for the attorney to gain your business but then, they might over bill you.

Some attorneys will bill hourly, with rates usually starting at $200 an hour and going up from there. If your attorney is planning on taking an hourly approach, be sure you have an understanding of how incremental times will be billed. Some attorneys bill in 15 minute increments, so even a quick 5 minute conversation will be billed for a full 15 minutes.

Alternatively, the attorney can use a flat fee approach. For real estate transactions, I believe that it is in your favor to take a flat fee approach, or even a percentage of the purchase price, so that you may avoid unpleasant surprises later in your bill. This is because if an attorney charges you on an hourly basis, you may have no idea how much time they are actually spending on your transaction and they can easily over charge you. On the contrary, when you are billed on a flat fee basis, you can have a clear expectation of what services are provided in that flat fee and can rest assured that you are only being billed for the work you want done.

Additionally, one mistake I see many sellers make is that they fail to realize that when they engage the attorney in conversation that is not related to the case at hand, the attorney is billing for that time. As a general rule, keep the conversations limited to the case and not about unrelated topics such as how much you may dislike the buyer's agent.

3.   How do you typically handle a real estate transaction?

Any experienced real estate attorney should be able to give you an overview of the necessary action steps needed. At this time, you may also want to discuss the roles and tasks you expect of the attorney so that there are no misunderstandings later on. Specifically, you can ask the attorney to limit their involvement in certain ways. For seasoned real estate attorneys, they often understand that each real estate transaction is unique and requires a different approach. For example, one transaction may require the review of a contract and handling negotiations while another will only require the review of closing documents.

As part of understanding how the transaction will be handled, you will also want to be clear about who will be working on your transaction. For example, although you may have met with the principal attorney during your initial consultation, this does not necessarily mean that the same attorney will be handling all parts of the transaction. In fact, in larger firms, it is common practice to give the initial parts of the work to a paralegal or newer attorney to handle and then have the more seasoned attorney handle any direct interactions with the client. If this is how the law firm of your choosing handles their cases, be sure that you feel comfortable with this. This is because the real estate transaction has many deadlines that need to be met, and if more than one person is involved, it may mean that there is a higher likelihood that something can fall through the cracks.

4.   When are you available?

Finally, it is worth asking when the real estate attorney will be available to you. Real estate transactions can be incredibly time sensitive.

Imagine if you were to receive an offer at 8 pm on a Friday evening and then have to wait until Monday morning to hear back from your attorney — for most prospective buyers, this would not be acceptable. Specifically, you should ask what their turnaround time is from receiving an offer to reviewing it and advising you, as this will be critical information that your prospective buyer will want to know. In fact, as mentioned earlier, some buyers will place an expiration date on their offer in order to make sure that you will move quickly in giving them a response as to whether or not you accept their offer.

As such, you will want to know if the attorney will offer extended hours and whether or not they are willing to work during the weekend. You may even ask whether or not they are willing to share their cell phone number with you so that you can get a hold of them during non-normal working hours in case an urgent matter arises.

Now, once you have interviewed a handful of attorneys, it's time to make a decision!

When you circle back with your winning attorney, you will be expected to sign a document referred to as a Retainer Agreement or Letter of Engagement, which will highlight the terms of services you can expect from your attorney. In the Retainer Agreement, expect to have a complete description of the transaction for which legal representation is sought, a complete list of duties and services that will be performed by the attorney, as well as a detailed account of how much, how often, and in what manner payment will be made (check, credit, or cash). The Agreement will also highlight what additional costs and expenses you will be responsible for including any filing fees, travel, printing, and other services. Additionally, the Agreement will outline how and when the Agreement terminates — perhaps you can terminate at any time or reason, but also take note of when the attorney can terminate the Agreement. Often times an attorney will terminate when there is non-cooperation or non-payment by you.

Once you have signed the Retainer Agreement, you should have an in depth conversation with your attorney about what factors are most important to you during the sale of your home. Here is a list of common questions the attorney may ask:

- Do you want to make sure the sale is done as quickly as possible or would you prefer to have some delays so that you may find your next home?
- Are you the heir or executor of a property whose owner is now deceased?
- Do you know whether you will be out of town and therefore need a Power of Attorney drafted?
- Is the property in some state of distress? For example, are you selling due to a divorce or possible foreclosure?
- Do you own the property with a non-cooperative owner?
- Are you aware of any judgments or liens against the property?

All of these factors are incredibly important for your attorney to know in order to facilitate a smooth real estate closing. Of course, no one can guarantee a smooth settlement — in fact, I believe that Murphy's Law of "Anything that can go wrong will go wrong" plays a strong role in real estate transactions. Real estate transactions can be complicated by having to navigate specific rules and regulations, all while having to manage the emotional toll that many buyers and sellers experience. However, engaging the services of a knowledgeable attorney from the onset can most definitely help. Besides, I think we can all agree that it is pretty cool to be able to say,

> **"Let me first discuss that with my attorney."**

Now that we know the role that a real estate attorney plays within the real estate transaction and have a list of critical questions that need to be asked before hiring one, let's move on to the next chapter where we will discuss the role of a title company.

CHAPTER NINETEEN

❖

CHOOSING THE RIGHT PROFESSIONAL: THE TITLE COMPANY

Remember when you purchased your very first home? Remember when the agent (or attorney) turned to you and asked which title company you would be using? Well, if you are anything like most of my buyers, chances are that you probably had no idea what a title company even was before that point. And I don't blame you, considering the fact that deciding which title company to use is usually one of the last concerns a purchaser has. However, as you are probably now aware having gone through the purchase experience, the role of the title company is actually incredibly important as they help facilitate a smooth closing.

When it comes to choosing a title company, the seller technically has no input as to which company the buyer decides to use due to the Real Estate Settlement Procedures Act (RESPA), which is a law that was passed in 1974.

The main objective of RESPA was to help facilitate a more transparent way of conducting real estate transactions by requiring lenders, mortgage brokers, and title companies to provide borrowers with pertinent and timely disclosures regarding the nature and costs of the real estate settlement process. The act was also designed to prohibit potentially abusive practices such as kickbacks and referral fees.

As to how it relates to home sellers, according to RESPA, "No seller of property that will be purchased with the assistance of a federally related mortgage loan shall require, directly or indirectly, as a condition to selling the property, that title insurance covering the property be purchased by the buyer from any particular title company." Therefore, although the seller may want the buyer to use a particular title company, if the buyer is receiving a federally issued loan, which is usually the case, the seller may not dictate which title company the buyer chooses. In fact, doing so comes with some hefty consequences, as the penalty for violating this provision is an amount equal to three times the cost of the title insurance provided.

Therefore, instead of the seller dictating which title company will be used, the generally accepted business practice in most jurisdictions is for the buyer's agent to recommend a handful of title companies to the buyer, and then allowing the buyer to decide which title company they want to hire. Usually, both the buyer and seller are indifferent in regards to the title company used, but most real estate agents will have a preferred title company or settlement agent. This preference usually stems from the fact that title companies, so long as they abide by the strict RESPA rules and regulations, can help with some of the marketing costs that real estate agents incur and therefore, their relationship becomes an "I'll scratch your back if you scratch mine." For example, if an agent refers their clients to a specific title company, then that title company will be more inclined to cover some marketing expenses for the agent which is why the buyer's agent will want their buyer to use their recommended title company.

Now although a seller's hands are usually tied in regards to which title company the buyer chooses, there are still four general questions that I strongly urge sellers to ask the title company, well in advance of settlement.

1. *How much will this cost me?*

First, a seller should ask a real estate attorney or agent what the usual and customary fees are that they can reasonably expect to pay to the title company. While one might think the buyer would bear all the costs associated with the title company, this line of thinking is incorrect. Responsibility in the costs associated with title insurance varies state to state and sometimes, even from one county to the next.

For example, in the state of Texas, the seller customarily bears the burden of paying the owner's title policy. Alternatively, in the state of

Maryland, the buyer usually pays for both the owner's insurance policy and the lender's insurance policy. But of course, all of this can be negotiated, too. As such, you will want to know what is typical in your state so that you can include this in your net sheet when determining what your expected profits will be from the sale.

It is also important to note that title insurance rates are set by statutes, which means that the fee is pre-determined based on the size of the buyer's loan, and varies depending on the state in which the property is located. The good news is that the premium that needs to be paid is only a one-time fee, and it is not an ongoing expense. The bad news is that although the insurance premium to be paid is bound by what the statute dictates, each title company can still tack on its own set of additional service fees. These fees can include recordation, wiring, copy, attorney, and settlement fees. These additional fees can quickly add up, and if you are not familiar with what you are reasonably expected to pay as the seller, then you could leave yourself open to having to pay unnecessary fees. As such, it would be prudent to not only be aware of fees that a seller is customarily expected to pay, and the applicable law in the state, but also be aware of the fees charged by the specific title company that the prospective buyer has chosen. If the title company tries to include additional fees that are not customary for your state, tell them so! By getting ahead of the issue before you have a ratified offer, you can greatly reduce your chances of having to deal with last minute unexpected (and sometimes, unreasonable) title fees. Or, you could even include a provision within the Purchase Agreement that expressly states that any fees charged to the seller by the title company will be the responsibility of the purchaser.

Again, just about anything is negotiable in real estate!

---

2.   Will you be able to meet the proposed settlement date deadline?

Confirm that the buyer's proposed settlement date is feasible. For example, if an eager buyer proposes settlement to be in a week, you will want to confirm with the title company that everything will be done before then, as opposed to having to hire movers and get everything ready on your end, only to be disappointed when the title company comes back stating that they need more time. Speaking of which, most title companies, assuming there are no surprises such as judgments or liens that pop up when the title abstract is returned, should be able to provide title insurance in about a week or two. This is why it can be wise for you to have your attorney pull a preliminary title search before placing the property on the market. Pulling a title search can cost between $100 - $200, but it is an investment that can be well worth it, since it will allow you to resolve any issues that you may or may not been aware of before the buyer does. If you leave it for the buyer to discover, depending on what your Purchase Agreement stipulates, the buyer may not be legally bound to stick around and wait for you to clear the issue and they can walk away from the sale without losing their earnest money deposit.

Also, as a general rule of thumb, there are certain days that you may not want settlement to even fall on. Title companies have some days in which they are busier than others and as we all know, when any individual or company feels slightly overwhelmed, things may be overlooked and when it comes to your settlement, this is never a good thing. Title companies are busiest during the last week of the month so, if possible, try to avoid having to close that week. Additionally, since Fridays are the bank's busiest days, as these are paydays, financial intuitions are usually pretty busy so again, you may want to try to avoid settling on Fridays. Finally, another time you will want to avoid settlement are the two weeks out of the year in which property taxes are due, as this can make it tricky for prorating the appropriate debits and credits for the sellers and buyers.

3. *Will you provide me with ample time to review all of the documents?*

As of October 2015, the Consumer Financial Protection Bureau

(CFPB) ruled that lenders (and therefore the title company) must deliver the Closing Disclosure (CD) to the consumer at least three business days prior to the date of consummation of the transaction. As such, if a settlement is scheduled for Thursday, then the CD must be delivered on Monday to the purchaser. In some cases, when a change occurs between the time the CD is given and closing, then there will be an additional three business days tacked on to allow everyone to review the documents. The three-day rule was passed to help the consumer so that they have ample time to address any concerns. There are exceptions as to which changes are allowed to occur without having to wait an additional three days, but they are very rare.

With this information in mind, it would not be unreasonable for the seller to receive their side of the paperwork at the same time as the buyer. As such, when you call and speak with the title company, you will want to let them know that you want ample time to go over and review all the paperwork. By letting the title company know that you expect to stay abreast with the process, you can increase your chances of a smooth settlement.

On this note, let the title company know ahead of time if you are planning on using the proceeds of the sale to purchase a new home, as is often the case. In fact, if you are purchasing a new home after the sale of your current home within the same state, it would make matters a lot smoother if you used the same title company that was handling the sale to also handle the purchase of your new home.

4. Will you travel to a mutually agreeable location for settlement?

The final suggestion I would make is that if you receive an offer that includes the name of a title company whose office is located further away from the property than you would be willing to travel to, it would be prudent to have your agent or attorney confirm that the title company would be willing to travel to accommodate all parties on the day of settlement. Trust me when I say that this has been a big point of contention as settlement draws closer and the sellers realize that they would have to go completely out of their way on the day of settlement.

As such, you may want to reach out to the title company and get clarification on their protocol in allowing you to pre-sign the documents, which was covered in Chapter Ten. You may also want to know whether or not they offer the option to allow you to sign electronically, laws permitting. As of now, many states require a "wet ink" signature, whereby the parties to a document must sign their names with their own hands upon a paper document by ink pen — specifically blue ink. In fact, even if a traditionally wet ink signature is then scanned, that scanned version is no longer deemed to be a "wet ink." Therefore, some jurisdictions will not allow a document to be electronically signed. However, in today's market, many title companies offer mobile services, which allow the settlement agent to travel to a location that is most convenient for the buyer and seller, so be sure to have this conversation with the title company before accepting an offer.

THE ROLE OF THE TITLE COMPANY

The main role of the title company is to facilitate the transaction, which means they are in charge for, generally speaking, six crucial elements of the entire sale.

1. Issuance of Clean Title

One of the main roles of the title company is to ensure that the home seller is giving the new homebuyer clean title. What is "clean" title? In short, the title company will want to conduct a title search (also known as an abstract of title), which is a thorough examination of property records in order to confirm that the seller (an individual, a couple, joint owners, or a company) is the actual and rightful owner and that there is no one else that has any claim to the property.

In conducting a title search, the title company will want to watch out for any types of liens against the property. A lien acts as a notice to the world communicating that a creditor is claiming that you owe them money and, as such, they are ensuring the payment of that debt by using the property as the collateral against the amount owed.

There are generally three main types of liens. The first is called a mechanic's lien, which allows contractors who have done work on your home to file a lien on the property in an amount that is equivalent to the cost of the home repair. Another common type of lien is a judgment lien, which allows the winning party of a court case to place a lien against the property. Finally, there are tax liens that can be placed against the property if you do not pay your federal, state, or county taxes.

Liens are public information since they are generally filed with the county records office or state agency, and therefore, it is the duty of the title company to find any outstanding liens. If they find a lien, this will impact the sale of your home, as there will be a hold on the sale until the issue is resolved. As such, if you are thinking of selling your home, you may want to pay off any debts that you are aware of before placing the home on the market as to not hold up the sale. By getting ahead of the problem, you can begin resolving the issue and begin repayment. In fact, it is incredibly beneficial for you (or preferably your attorney) to try to negotiate the judgment down before placing the property on the market. This is because if you wait until you are under contract and the title company contacts the creditor, you will automatically lose your negotiation advantage, since you are now coming from a place of desperation in order to settle on your home and, therefore, the creditor will be less inclined to negotiate. Usually, the repayment comes out of the proceeds of the sale of the house, which is why it is important to notify the title company of any liens that you are aware of as soon as possible.

However, if you discover that a lien has been placed on the property after you are already under contract, you may want to act quickly to resolve the debts as to not hold up the sale of your property. You can also refuse to pay, or contest the lien — but not without consequence.

If you decide to refuse payment or contest, depending on the terms of your contract, the buyer may be entitled to walk away from the sale without losing their earnest money deposit. This is because mortgage companies will not finance a property until there is clean title. Alternatively, the buyer can decide to pay the debt in order to move forward with the sale, but this is rare since often times, a buyer will have only saved up just enough money to cover a down payment and closing costs.

2. Property Survey

The title company may also be required to conduct a property survey, depending on whether or not the lender requires it. A property survey calculates precisely where your property begins and where is ends, also known as boundary lines. This is a critical piece of information for a new buyer, as they may want to erect fences, pave driveways, or build additions to the property. Furthermore, a property survey will reveal all the conditions imposed by law, such as easements, which can give a neighbor the right to use a piece of your property.

3. Calculations and Prorations

The title company is also responsible for making sure that the buyer and seller proportionately divide the costs of certain taxes and bills up to the date of settlement. Typically, a title company will prorate the property taxes, interest, insurance, homeowner's association fees, condo fees, water bills and other utility bills. As the home seller, you will want to make sure these numbers are accurate with the time of settlement, and that you are being credited for any bills you previously paid for.

4. Title Insurance

The title company will also prepare the insurance commitment for two different types of policies, including the Lender's Insurance Policy and the Owner's Insurance Policy. If the buyer is receiving a loan to purchase the home, the lender will always require a Lender's Policy, which will solely protect the bank's interests. Alternatively, the Owner's Policy may be purchased at settlement, which will provide the new owner with protection.

Title insurance protects the lenders or owners against any financial loss as well as payment of legal costs to defend any unforeseen claims and/or fraud that may arise from disputes over the ownership of the property. For example, assume you purchase a property but then after ten years of living there and always paying your mortgage on time, someone named Ken comes forward with a legitimate claim as the rightful owner of the home. In such circumstances, the title search may have missed something but the title insurance will kick in and will likely either pay you or Ken the value of the home to resolve the issue.

5.   Legal Documents Needed for Closing

The title company is also responsible for preparing certain legal documents. In preparing these documents, it is important for you to understand that since the attorney working for the title company does not represent either of the parties, the lawyer must take the contract as he or she finds it. What this means is that since a contract can sometimes contain vague and ambiguous — or even sometime conflicting — terms, the attorney is not authorized to answer any questions regarding the interpretations of the contract. Instead, the lawyer must turn to the parties of the contract for the proper interpretations.

6.   Conducting the Closing

The title company is also responsible for conducting the settlement. Depending on where you live, either all the parties involved will gather around or, if this is not feasible or if the transaction was a particularly difficult one where emotions ran high, the sellers and buyers may request to have separate signing meetings. For you, since you are the seller, I would recommend that you request to sign your documents beforehand because sellers will have significantly less paperwork to review and sign than the buyer. As such, you can get in and out much quicker since you will not need to wait around for the buyer to have to sign their portion of the documents.

In some states, it is required to have an attorney conduct the settlement while in other states, a settlement agent who is a Notary Public can conduct the settlement. Either way, settlement can last anywhere between one or more hours, depending on whether the buyers and sellers want to read every single document they are signing, which of course, is their prerogative. After all, you are signing incredibly important documents! However, and unfortunately so, I have sometimes witnessed the closing agent or attorney try to rush the process since they may have another scheduled settlement for that same day. But it is important for you to not feel rushed and to take your time in reviewing these critical documents.

Either way, you should note that the agent or attorney is a neutral third party only. As such, they cannot give legal advice or interpret any documents for you. The closing attorney/agent can explain each item and review how the numbers were calculated, but for any legal opinions, you will want to consult with your own attorney.

Now, although in Chapter Ten we discussed what could happen if you were unable to attend settlement, it is worth reminding you that when you are selling your home, you really need to consider whether or not you will be available on the date of settlement. This is an incredibly important detail to pay close attention to since a minor oversight can be disastrous to your goal of selling. This is why it is so important to at least understand the basics of a Power of Attorney Agreement. As such, please be sure to check out the free video mini course I have created for additional insight, which can be found at www.sellyourhomewithconfidencebook.com/course.

Now, as part of conducting a smooth settlement, you should note which documents you will be expected to bring with you. Depending on whether you are selling your home as an individual, corporation, or as a representative for an estate, you will be required to bring different documents.

Individual
- Driver's License
- 2nd Form of Identification (passport, credit card with photo, work ID)

- Original Power of Attorney (if applicable)
- Wiring Instructions (if applicable)
  - Bank Name
  - Bank Address
  - Routing Number
  - Account Number

Corporate Entities - If you are selling through a business, you will typically need to provide the following information at least 1 week before closing:
- Articles of Incorporation or Organization
- Operating Agreement, Amendments, and Bylaws
- Resolution stating who has authority to sign on behalf of the company
- A roster of all current members
- Certificate of Good Standing — Must be valid within 30 or 60 days, depending on the rules of the title company.

Estate Sales - If you are the Personal Representative of an estate, you must provide the following information at least 1 week before closing:
- Letters of Administration
- Death Certificate
- Accounting
- Will
- List of Heirs

Once all parties have signed, assuming there are proceeds from the sale and you did not have to sell as a short sale, you will either receive a check or have the funds wired to you. At this point, the buyer will also receive all keys to the house, any garage door openers, and security system codes.

7. Recordation of Documents

The final responsibility of the title company is making sure that all the documents are properly recorded in the courthouse, such as the new deed, mortgage documents, and Power of Attorney Agreements. The title company will also make sure that all the proper vendors have been paid, assuming that was previously agreed upon as part of the responsibility of the title company, such as paying the termite company or surveyor.

Now, congratulations! You have successfully sold your home!

But before we wrap up, I truly believe that this book would not be complete without a discussion of the National Association of REALTORS® (NAR). In the following and final chapter, I would like to take a close look at the NAR and to provide you with my parting thoughts on the real estate industry and how the information you have just learned in this book can spearhead a massive change within the entire real estate industry!

CHAPTER TWENTY

❖

CONCLUDING THOUGHTS

Unmistakably, the motive of the National Association of REALTORS® (NAR), the only trade association for the entire industry, is purely concerned with lining its own pockets and not the well-being of the people they are intended to serve — and therein lies one of the largest contributing pitfalls of the entire real estate industry. The real estate industry is sinking at a pace unlike any time before and I believe that the NAR and everything it stands for, or lack thereof, is the main contributing factor.

Before I dive into the many ways that I feel that the NAR is failing its own members, I do believe it is worth mentioning how the NAR has helped push forward a few wins for consumers. For example, the NAR is credited for extending the First-Time Homebuyer Tax Credit back in 2008, which provided financial incentives for first time home buyers back when the market was still feeling the impacts of the housing bubble burst. Additionally, the NAR has convinced government agencies such as the Federal Housing Administration (FHA) and the U.S. Department of Housing and Urban Development (HUD) to relax their credit standards in more recent years. However, it remains that as the perceived leader of the real estate industry, I strongly believe that the NAR has a duty to place an even stronger focus on creating more value for those who keep the members in business — you!

One clear way in which the NAR could have helped consumers more but did not can be illustrated back in 2005 when the Department of Justice (DOJ) filed an antitrust lawsuit against NAR. During this time, there was a growing popularity of the Internet, and the DOJ alleged that NAR was limiting access of the Multiple Listing Service (MLS) to internet-based competitors (such as Zillow and Trulia) who were providing more transparency to consumers.

For those of you unfamiliar with the MLS, it is a database and software that is governed by the NAR and may only be accessed by those who either pay a membership fee to the NAR or to licensed agents. As such, it is used by real estate brokers/agents who are representing sellers to share information about a property that is listed for sale so that other brokers/agents may show these properties to potential buyers. Therefore, the NAR was limiting competition against those Internet-based competitors who were disrupting the traditional real estate model (like Zillow and Trulia) by using the Internet instead of the MLS.

Although the case was settled in 2008 when the NAR agreed to change the policies that restrained competition, it is still a reminder of everything that is wrong with the real estate industry; the inherent lack of transparency and the overly powerful trade association who wants to restrict information under lock and key when that information should be readily available to consumers.

Today, the mission of the NAR is "to help its members become more profitable and successful," by "influencing and shaping the real estate industry"; advocating for "the right to own, use and transfer real property"; and "developing standards for efficient and ethical real estate business practices." However, if this was truly their mission, then they should start with demanding a higher barrier of entry into their organization. In fact, in order to become a member of the NAR, one must only take a one to two hour "course" which discusses the Code of Ethics and pay their exorbitant membership dues. Thus, with the pathetically low barrier of entry, the NAR is nothing more than an organization that neither has the correct methodology nor the teeth to pursue its stated goals of furthering the integrity of the profession. Instead, their only true mission is to block certain policies and developments in an effort to keep its members relevant in an industry foiled with negative reputation that is so desperately crying for reform — just as we saw with the antitrust lawsuit back in 2005.

Now, exactly how powerful is the NAR? NAR's political action committee (PAC) is considered one of the most formidable lobbying efforts in the country, and the largest contributor of direct contributions to federal candidates to develop, advance, and implement the association's monetary objectives.

So, how does all of this impact the sale of your home?

Think of it this way: when the largest trade association in the United States is using about 42% of its members' annual dues towards lobbying efforts, you can guarantee that they are pressing Congress to write laws that are in their favor. In fact, if something in your real estate transaction goes awry, I can guarantee you that the laws that the NAR is so strongly lobbying towards will not protect you, instead, those laws are meant to keep the REALTOR® in business. Laws that will continue to try and keep the consumer dependent on the real estate professional.

And of course, the NAR will continue to survive as it keeps its barrier to entry low and its membership dues high. As such, the NAR will continue with its true mission of preserving its own existence while fattening the pockets of its executives. To prove this point, I will once again refer to Simon Sinek, the author of the book, <u>Leaders Eat Last</u>, who wrote:

> *"If our leaders are to enjoy the trappings of their position in the hierarchy, then we expect them to offer us protection. The problem is, for many of the overpaid leaders, we know that they took the money and perks and didn't offer protection to their people. In some cases, they even sacrificed their people to protect or boost their own interests. This is what so viscerally offends us. We only accuse them of greed and excess [because] we feel they have violated the very definition of what it means to be a leader. "*

Now, in the case of the NAR, the supposed leader of the real estate industry, I believe that they do in fact sacrifice their members for their own monetary interests. And like it or not, that leadership style trickles down from the REALTORS® and onto the home sellers. This is because when leaders mislead their own people, regardless of the impetus, bad things manifest as the members' behavior begins to adapt and mirror the leaders' style. This is evidenced by the poor decisions some REALTORS® have made by placing their self-interests above their

145

clients' interests as discussed throughout this book.

Of course, I find this to be incredibly backwards since as we saw in Chapter Thirteen of this book, by becoming a member of the NAR and therefore a REALTOR®, it is supposed to be an indicator that the agent has agreed to a higher ethical standard than their mere real estate agent peers. However, as we discussed in that chapter, most consumers have no idea that these ethical standards even exist and therefore, in the eyes of the consumer, those who keep real estate professionals in business, there is no difference between an agent and the "high and mighty" REALTOR®.

In fact, this facade, that a REALTOR® adheres to a higher ethical standard, is just that: a facade. This is bolstered by the fact that often times, agents do not *choose* to become a member on their own accord, but rather they are *strong-armed* into becoming a member. One way that the NAR coerces agents into becoming members is due to the fact that the their rules and regulations stipulate that whenever the broker who owns or manages an office chooses to become a member, all of their agents under that brokerage have no choice but to also become a member. As such, while I adore the brokerage I am currently affiliated with, since my broker is a member of the NAR, I must be one, too. But, not because I want to. And not because I find any benefit to joining. And certainly, not because I believe it is going to automatically make me become more ethical since I was forced to agree to the REALTOR® Code of Ethics. Instead, I joined because I had no other choice but to join.

With this being said, I believe that the NAR needs to come to the realization that since they are essentially *requiring* their members to become affiliated as a means of being able to do business, they cannot expect their members to commit to their Code of Ethics. Instead, only people who make a commitment based on ***free-will and choice*** will uphold those values, as they willingly joined.

In fact, I firmly believe that if membership was not required or rather, that if the members were not forced into maintaining their membership, 99% of real estate agents would choose to forgo their membership completely. By requiring agents to be members, the NAR has destroyed the value of the membership, and therefore, it carries little to no true meaningful significance. If the NAR wants to accurately see how they are perceived or valued, then they should make membership truly voluntary. Only then will the terms "REALTOR®" hold any weight.

Further, a quick glance at the hundreds of real estate forums online will prove that there is a clear upward dissatisfaction among many of the members of NAR. One recurring common thread of dissatisfaction is seen with the flawed, money-hungry approach of the designations available within the association. Simply put, these designations are yet another mechanism used by the NAR to further their interests: to make money. Each designation not only costs hundreds of dollars to receive, but in order to retain the ability to continue using the designation, the REALTOR® must pay an annual recurring fee. Let's stop and think about that for a second. How does it make any sense for a person to have to, year after year, pay a fee for a designation they have already earned? In my opinion, this is the equivalent of a university charging its students a yearly fee to continue using their bachelor's degree on their resumes!

But tough times create an appetite for change and to shake up the status quo. And nowhere has this been truer than in the real estate industry. I cannot think of any other industry that has not listened to what the consumers are saying about what they want and yet still manages to survive. But the quicker everyone realizes the inherent flaws within the NAR, the closer we will be to changing the status quo within the real estate industry.

And this brings me to why I have decided to bring all of this to your attention — because I believe that it is the home seller who ultimately holds the power to make radical changes to the industry and the reason is simple: money.

> **It is the home seller who must pay the commissions that are earned within the real estate transaction and therefore, if and when home sellers decide that they want more training, more professionalism, and more transparency from their agents, only then can the industry as a whole be forced to change.**
>
> **And if there are more home sellers who are privy to the information that I have shared within these pages, then, and only then, can we make an impact, en masse, to the way the real estate industry is run as we will all fight to hold agents to a higher standard.**

But until real estate agents and the industry as a whole are held to a higher standard, it remains critical for you to conduct your own due diligence, which luckily, is exactly what you have done by reading this book.

As you have now come to realize, home sellers face significant risks in today's highly litigious society - whether there is just one misstep in disclosures of property conditions, premises liability, or discrimination, a home seller can find themselves party to a lawsuit. But now, having read this book, your ability to completely avoid or to at least *significantly* minimize your risk will not be difficult to do. With this book as your guide, it is my most heartfelt intention that you have been provided with all the tools you need to truly, Sell Your Home With Confidence!

ACKNOWLEDGEMENTS

❖

I want to give a special thank you to my dad. Many people don't know this, but my dad is the reason why I am in real estate in the first place. You see, after having graduated from law school and having little clue as to what direction I wanted to take my career in, it was my dad who agreed to let me help him purchase a new property - and all without even becoming a licensed real estate agent*! By allowing me to represent you, I was able to find my passion and purpose in life and for that, I thank you! But more importantly, without your support, I would have never been able to follow my dreams.

I also want to thank the people who have helped me along the way. The following people are the ones who are responsible for pushing me to stay focused, motivated, and who have always provided words of encouragement when I have needed it the most — my mom, my aunt, my sister, Brett Dieck, Angel Casas, and Renee Livshin. And last but certainly not least, I want to thank my long-time, childhood best friend, Golnaz Alemousavi who helped me with my very first round of edits.

Finally, I want to thank all of my clients who have entrusted me with the sale or purchase of their home. I believed that every sale is as unique as the home being sold, and I have found learning lessons in all of them.

From the bottom of my heart, I thank you!

---

*Attorneys do not need a real estate license to engage in the purchase or sale of real estate since by virtue of their law license, they are already equipped with the knowledge to buy and sell. A lawyer only needs to become licensed if they want to market that they handle real estate transactions and if they intend on doing more than a handful of transactions per year.

ABOUT SAMAN SABA

❖

Saman Saba is the owner and principal real estate attorney of the Saba Law Group, LLC. Her firm brings a holistic approach to real estate, as she is able to understand that each transaction can and usually does impact other areas of the law. For example, the sale of a home often also involves issues such as family law, bankruptcy law, immigration law, and/or trust and estates. As such, Saman and her team of attorneys are able to address those issues, too, which helps ensure that her clients' interests are protected from every angle of the law.

Saman graduated from University of Maryland with degrees in Political Science and Women's Studies and received her J.D. from University of Baltimore School of Law. Additionally, she holds a licenses as a REALTOR®, title insurance producer, certified mediator, and a notary public.

Saman also has an intense love for international travel, having now traveled to over 30 countries and counting! She also enjoys fitness, women empowerment, and is a lover all of all things peanut butter.

Please feel free to connect with Saman on the following social media sites:

Instagram: https://www.instagram.com/Iamsamansaba/
Facebook: https://www.facebook.com/SamanSabaEsq

WAIT! BEFORE YOU LEAVE ...

— ❖ —

From the bottom of my heart, I want to thank you for reading this book and I am excited for you as you can now Sell Your Home With Confidence. It is my hope that you enjoyed reading this book and that you have found it useful. If you did, I would be so appreciative if you would take a moment to write a short review on Amazon!

Reviews are crucial so that I can improve future editions.

Also, if you know of anyone who is thinking about selling their home, I encourage you to send them a copy of this book — whether you gift it to them on Amazon or even email them an electronic copy of the book, it makes no difference to me. I truly just want every home seller to have the right tools and information to reduce their liability, so that everyone can sell their home with confidence!

WANT MORE?

Please head over to my website to download bonuses, learn more about my other books, and to learn more about why I have decided to donate a portion of the proceeds from this book to go to Congenital Diaphragmatic Hernia (CDH) research!

http://bit.ly/sellwithconfidencebook

BONUS CHAPTER!!

——————— ❖ ———————

BE WARY OF THE STATISTICS

With a slogan like "What Happens in Vegas, Stays in Vegas," it is no surprise that the gambling mecca of the world has its fair share of crazy gambling stories that give heightened meaning to the expression, "put your money where your mouth is." For some, these stories are based on which cards are dealt — pure luck. Just walk into any casino and you will be able to quickly pick out who is winning based on luck. It's the guy who is pumping up the crowd around him with his fists in the air while squealing in delight; his energy is almost folkloric. He is remarkable to watch and the crowd absolutely LOVES him.

But for others, like professional poker players, those stories are based on skill and calculations. These professionals will tell you that poker is all about examining and studying a certain set of facts and trying to find situations where they have a statistical advantage. They are typically much more subdued, as they need to focus on the mathematics of probability — trying to determine the likelihood of a particular hand playing out in their favor. All the while, they need to decipher their opponents' "poker face." These professionals will tell you that there is a formula for success that is not based on luck.

And selling your house on your own, which is commonly known as being a For Sale By Owner (FSBO) works the same way — there is also a formula for success.

Recently, I had a chance to sit down with a FSBO client, we will call her Susan, who came to me for my legal services. As a real estate attorney, much like an agent, I review the offers that have been submitted by prospective buyers, I negotiate on the seller's behalf, and I continue to represent their financial and legal interests through the process — all the way to the settlement table. But unlike a typical agent, I utilize my legal knowledge to identify any potential legal problems BEFORE they turn into a legal nightmare for my clients.

In Susan's case, I was able to use both my attorney hat and my agent hat to help navigate the sale of her home. I was able to wear multiple hats because, although I was retained for my legal knowledge, I recognized the reason as to why the offer that was submitted to Susan was a low-ball offer only because of my knowledge as an agent. Susan shared with me that this offer was the *third* low-ball offer she had received and she couldn't understand why. Susan was clearly frustrated and was ready to accept the fact that she had no other choice but to take one of these low-ball offers. But I knew that, like most FSBOs I have worked with, Susan's problem was a marketing one. I was able to identify this because, as an agent, I know what goes into properly marketing a property in order to generate quality offers.

In fact, just one quick look at Susan's marketing materials and I was able to see that if she made a few tweaks here and there, she would not have to settle for a low-ball offer. So, what changes did we make to Susan's marketing? How did we take her current sub-par, flat marketing plan and transform it into a dynamic, three-dimensional, and not to mention, stellar one? How did we gain more eye-balls on the house while also gaining more prospective buyers and thus, higher quality offers?

I promise to share my formula for success (AKA marketing plan) but before I do, let's cover some general topics that require attention. Specifically, I want to debunk one of the biggest myths within the real estate industry. For many home sellers, they believe that in order to have a successful sale, they are required to work with a real estate agent. But the truth is, agents are only "required" by perception. Where does this perception come from? Personally, I blame the National Association of REALTORS® (NAR), who attempts to insulate sellers from the reality of the market — to have you believe that the odds are against you when you choose to sell your house on your own.

The NAR makes it incredibly discouraging for FSBOs, as it paints a pretty bleak picture for the success rate for FSBOs. *According to NAR's 2015 statistics, only 8% of U.S. homes were sold by a FSBO.* Now, I don't know about you, but I would **strongly** prefer that reports like this come from an independent source, rather than the NAR.

In my main book, *Sell Your Home With Confidence: Reduce Your Liability When Selling*, we established that the NAR's main purpose is to keep it's REALTOR® members in business which in turn, keeps them in business. It follows then that their data will be heavily weighted in favor of what they would prefer to relay to consumers so that their members would stay in business. Logically, it follows that statistics like the ones given by the NAR are analogous to when big tobacco companies would publish statements that misled consumers to believe that smoking was not as harmful as it truly was.

In any case, I would agree that FSBOs do not account for a large portion of the market. However, I also believe that the numbers are getting larger and the NAR is inaccurately reporting this upward trend. The NAR gives us no indication of how it is polling its data, which leads me to believe that it is defining a FSBO as someone who is not listed on the MLS. But even with that definition, the NAR would be misleading us, since there are indeed FSBOs who are also listed on the MLS, as there are plenty of sites that, for a fee, allow a home seller to market their home on the MLS.

Regardless of how the NAR has reached their calculations, one thing is clear, hiring a real estate agent to represent you is a choice and increasingly, I do believe more sellers are choosing to sell their home themselves. And unlike the NAR who will sometime spews inaccurate data with the hopes that it will discourage you from going the FSBO route, I am here to tell you that it is not an ***impossible*** task. However, while the task itself is not impossible, there is a formula for success when it comes to selling your home, just like playing poker. We will examine that formula for success in just a bit, but before we do, let's take a look at the real advantages and disadvantages of selling as a FSBO, which will help you decide whether selling as a FSBO is right for you.

WANT THE REST OF THIS BOOK?

TO FIND THIS BOOK
AND MANY OTHER RESOURCES
FOR HOME SELLERS,
PLEASE VISIT:

http://bit.ly/sellwithconfidencebook

www.ingramcontent.com/pod-product-compliance
Lightning Source LLC
Chambersburg PA
CBHW060603200326
41521CB00007B/645